VERBS, VERBS, VERBS

The Trickiest Action-Packed Words in English

by MARVIN TERBAN

SCHOLASTIC REFERENCE

To my wonderful Karen, who's not tricky but very action-packed!

Library of Congress Cataloging-in-Publication Data

Terban, Marvin.
    Verbs, verbs, verbs: the trickiest action-packed words in English / Marvin
      Terban
    p. cm. — (Scholastic guides)
    Includes index.
    Summary: Discusses irregular verbs, their tenses, and how
to use them and provides full conjugation of the 100 most
commonly used verbs.
    1. English language—Verb—Juvenile literature. 2. English lanugage—
Inflection—Juvenile literature. [1. English language—Verb.] I. Title. II. Series.
    PE1271 .T47 2002
    428.2—dc21
    2001057559

0-439-40156-9 (POB)
0-439-40164-X (PB)

10 9 8 7 6 5 4 3 2 1   02 03 04 05 06

Book design by Kay Petronio

Printed in the U.S.A.   60
First printing, August 2002

CONTENTS

1. **Kinds of Verbs** 5
What Is a Verb? 5
What Is a Sentence? 6
Helping Verbs 7
How Long Is a Verb? 8
Imperative Verbs 10
"You Understood" 11
The Verb "To Be" 12
Linking Verbs Link 13
What Is a Predicate? 14
Linking Verbs vs. Action
   Verbs 16

2. **More About Verbs** 19
Verb Tenses 19
Regular and
   Irregular Verbs 22
Tricky Verbs to Watch
   Out For 24
Principal Parts of Verbs 26
Active and Passive Voices 30
What is the Subject of a
   Sentence? 30

3. **Full Conjugations** 33
bite 34
break 36
bring 38
catch 40
choose 42
cut 44
draw 46
drive 48
feed 50
fight 52
fling 54
forget 56
forgive 58
freeze 60
give 62

hide 64
hold 66
know 68
see 70
seek 72
shake 74
sting 76
swing 78
teach 80
be 82

4. **More Irregular Verbs** 85
bear 87
beat 88
become 89
begin 90
bleed 91
blow 92
burst 93
buy 94
cling 95
come 95
cost 96
creep 96
deal 97
dive 98
do 99
drink 100
eat 101
fall 102
flee 103
fly 104
forbid 105
get 106
go 105
grind 108
grow 109
hang 110
have 111

..............................112
urt 113
keep..............................114
lay..............................115
lead..............................116
leave 117
lend 118
let..............................119
lie..............................120
lose 121
pay..............................122
put..............................123
read 124
rid 125
ride 126
ring..............................127
rise..............................128
run..............................129
say 130
set..............................131
shine..............................132
shoot 133
show..............................134
shrink..............................135
sing..............................136

slay 137
sleep..............................138
slide..............................139
speak..............................140
spin 141
spring..............................142
stand 143
steal..............................144
stick..............................145
stink 146
stride 146
strike 147
strive 148
swear..............................149
swim..............................150
take 151
tear 152
think..............................153
throw..............................154
wake..............................155
wear..............................156
wring 157
write 158
Index 159

CHAPTER ONE

KINDS OF VERBS

HELPING • IMPERATIVE • "TO BE" • LINKING

WHAT IS A VERB?

A verb is a word that shows or expresses action, being, or doing.

From the moment you woke up this morning to right now, you've used hundreds of verbs. You've spoken them, read them, heard them, and written them. You couldn't communicate with people without verbs. You couldn't even talk to a dog without them!

Every sentence must have a verb.

WHAT IS A SENTENCE?

Here's the world's best definition of a sentence: *A sentence is a group of words that contains a subject and a verb and that makes complete sense.* No verb, no sentence.

A sentence could be as short as one word, but that one word has to be a verb. "Stop!" is a sentence because the word *stop* is a verb. (For more about one-verb sentences, see "Imperative Verbs" on page 10.)

Most verbs show action.

Jennifer *leaped* over the snoozing elephant.

David *will jog* all the way to Walla Walla.

Lisa *should have eaten* the fried grasshoppers for dessert.

But "action" doesn't always mean fast-moving, energetic, vigorous, forceful, action-packed action like running, throwing, or jumping. (Whew! That last sentence was so full of action, it was exhausting.)

Some verbs show doing (calm action).

Some actions are quiet, still, or peaceful like sitting, dreaming, or breathing. (Now that's more restful, isn't it?) A verb can express just doing something—something that's not so active.

Chandranath *is looking* at the kitten in the tulip garden.

Karen softly *whispered* the silly secret in his left ear.

Blanca *will think* about the polka dot cushions tomorrow.

A verb can show being.

Being has no action in it at all. The verb "of being" (which is also called the verb "to be") doesn't do anything. It just shows that someone or something exists.

For more about the verb "to be," see page 12.

Action Verbs

Nilda *skipped* rope for two hours straight.

Jed *wrestled* the bear to a draw.

Xiao-Hang *pitched* a no-hitter again.

Doing Verbs (quiet actions)

Marcy *imagined* she was riding her bike in Otis.

Miss Konikowski *dreams* about math all night.

The raccoon *sleeps* in the barn.

Being Verbs

I *am* the greatest wizard in the universe.

They *were* in the organic food shop.

Peaches *is* a lap cat.

Here's a sentence that contains an action verb, a doing (calm action) verb, and a being verb in that order.

⌐action⌐   ⌐doing⌐
Jade *dashed* to the tree, *listened* to the baby birds, and
was very happy.
⌐being⌐

HELPING VERBS

There are twenty-three special verbs that help the main verbs express action, being, and doing. They are called helping or auxiliary verbs ("auxiliary" means "helping").

Here's an easy way to remember them:

3 begin with **B**	be	being	been
3 begin with **D**	do	does	did
3 begin with **M**	may	must	might
3 begin with **H**	have	has	had
3 end with **–ould**	could	would	should
2 end with **–ll**	shall	will	
5 are the verb "**to be**"	am, are, is, was, were		
Put them all into a **can**.	can		

Sometimes helping verbs help **add emphasis** to what you're saying.

> I definitely *do want* that little raincoat for my pet
>   gerbil.
>
> Sasha *must leave* this melting igloo immediately!
>
> Monica *should speak* softly next to the nervous gorilla.
>
> Mike *shall get* a haircut today, or no allowance for him.

Some helping verbs help to **express doubt or uncertainty**.

> Helene *may go* mountain-climbing if it doesn't rain.
>
> If Joseph can roll doughnuts, he *might get* the job.

Sometimes helping verbs help **ask questions**.

> *Did* Antonio just *burp* in Spanish in Spanish class?
>
> *Does* your dog always *snore* like that?
>
> *Will* it *be* okay if I ride my moped in your kitchen?
>
> *Are* you *walking* to Florida or flying?

Sometimes helping verbs and the word *not* help **make negative state-
ments**.

> Laurie *does* not *eat* green food, ever!
>
> They *do* not *juggle* swords at the school assembly.
>
> We *didn't walk* down the up staircase. (Note: "-n't" is
>   the contraction for "not.")

Other helping verbs help **express the tenses**. (For more about verb
tenses, see page 19.)

> Present tense: I *am studying* the Hundred Years' War in
>   history, and it *is taking* a hundred years to study it!
>
> Future tense: Glenn *will speak* backward on Tuesday.
>
> Present perfect tense: Kurt *has left* the planet for the
>   weekend.
>
> Past perfect tense: Bonnie *had been warned* about this
>   squirrel.

How Long Is a Verb?

A complete verb in a sentence can be one, two, three, or four words
long.

One-word Verbs

A verb can be just one word long.

> Margo *played* the glockenspiel in the school band.
>
> Jen *creates* fabulous jewelry at the tattoo parlor.
>
> Tim *built* fantastic birdhouses on the island.

Verb Phrases

A complete verb could also be a phrase of two, three, or four words depending on how many helping verbs there are in the verb phrase.

Two-word Verb Phrases

(one helping verb + one main verb)

> Fran *can climb* the greasy flagpole another day.
>
> You *will eat* the dinner that Nicola *has cooked*, or else!
>
> I *do like* Shelley's pet orangutang, honestly.
>
> Norma and Harry *must read* "Squealing Pigs Eat Alaska."
>
> They *were singing* loudly while Dr. Soghoian *was trying* to sleep.
>
> Peter *had danced* the hokey-pokey for hours.
>
> Juan really *should go* home now.

Three-word Verb Phrases

(two helping verbs + one main verb)

> The scenery for the show *is being painted* right now.
>
> My aunt *should have baked* this pie a little longer.
>
> The chickens *had been seen* near the golf course.
>
> Arnold *will be punished* for this.

Four-word Verb Phrases

(three helping verbs + one main verb)

> Mrs. Penn *could have been shoveling* the snow all this time.
>
> Anthony *must have been kidding* when he told you that.
>
> Steve *may have been playing* his tuba in the concert.

Verb Phrases Interrupted

The helping verbs and the main verb can be all together in a row, as in the sentences on page 9, or they can be interrupted by other words, as in the sentences below.

John *must have* absentmindedly *forgotten* his shoes at the dentist's.

Kate *could* easily *understand* his unhappiness at having lost the hiccupping contest.

Cindy *should have* immediately *stopped* the hot-air balloon.

We *can* never *allow* Sue in here again wearing that bunny costume.

Mrs. Potter *would have been* energetically *dancing* the hula by then.

IMPERATIVE VERBS

What Is an Imperative Verb?

An imperative verb is a special verb that **gives commands** or **makes requests**. People use imperative verbs all day long. You've probably used a few yourself today.

Go to your room, you ludicrous lout.

Kid, *catch* this artichoke.

Stop yodeling this instant!

Please *pass* the donkey food.

Class, *open* your books to page 97,843.

Notice that the imperative verb can be shouted angrily— "*Leave!*"—or expressed politely— "*Kindly **remove** that banana from your ear, sir.*"

One-word Sentences

A complete sentence could be as short as one word if that one word is an imperative verb. *Help!* is a complete sentence.

Are you wondering what the subject of the sentence "*Help!*" is? It's "You." What you're really saying is, "Would you please help me." But sometimes people leave out words when they give orders and make requests, especially if they're in a hurry, in trouble, or upset. The subject of an imperative verb is called "you understood." The word *you* really isn't in the sentence, but the reader or listener understands that "you" is the subject. Understand?

You often find imperative verbs on signs that give orders.

Hold on to the rail.

Count your change carefully.

Place your orders here.

Step into the car when the doors open.

Stand behind the white line.

Look both ways before you cross.

Cross at the green, not in between.

Sentences with imperative verbs can even tell you what not to do.

Don't run.

Never cheat.

Do not dribble.

One of the most famous sentences of the twentieth century contained two imperative verbs, and it was the same verb used twice.

"Ask not what your country can do for you—ask what you can do for your country."

—John F. Kennedy (1917–1963),
thirty-fifth president of the United States,
in his Inaugural Address on January 20, 1961

Other speakers and writers have used imperative verbs to good effect.

"Make the most of yourself, for that is all there is of you."

—Ralph Waldo Emerson (1803–1882),
American writer and philosopher

"Eat, drink, and be merry, for tomorrow ye diet."

> — *William Gilmore Beymer (1881-1969),
> American writer*

*"Let the people know the truth and the country is
safe."*

> — *Abraham Lincoln (1809-1865),
> sixteenth president of the United States*

THE VERB "TO BE"

"To be" is a very special verb. You could not do without it. You say, write, or hear the verb "to be" hundreds of times each day.

"To be" doesn't show action. It shows being and existing. It doesn't show that the subject of the sentence does, did, or will do anything. It just shows that the subject is, was, will be, has been, had been, or will have been.

Action verb: *The flamingo plopped into the mud puddle.*

Being verb: *The stuffed hippo was in the cookie jar.*

> **The verb "to be" is also called the verb of being.**

The Whole Verb "To Be" in Eight Words

The verb "to be" in all its tenses takes 114 words to say or write. (For the full conjugation of the verb "to be," see page 82.) But a quick way to remember this important verb is to learn just the following eight words: **am, are, is, was, were, be, being, been.** That's the verb "to be" in a nutshell.

MR. C.L.T.

A Little Play with the Verb "To Be"

Scene: A spaceship

Characters: Captain, Co-captain, Human Kid 1, Human Kid 2, and a Creature

Time: Far in the future

CAPTAIN: I **am** the fearless captain of the starcruiser *Wobbly,* and we **are** on a journey to outer space.

HUMAN KID 1: Aghhh! Who *is* that?

CAPTAIN: He *was* once a hideous, revolting, ugly, monstrous, disgusting, repulsive creature from a distant planet.

CO-CAPTAIN: We *were* afraid of him, but starting today he will *be* our C.L.T. (creature language translator).

CREATURE: Thank you, beautiful humans, for *being* so nice and friendly to an alien.

HUMAN KID 2: It has *been* a pleasure meeting you, Mr. C.L.T., we think.

CREATURE: Gizma hootchik xxup flujgee mookul. (Translation: The pleasure *is* all mine, I think.)

"To Be": Helping Verb or Main Verb? Both!

"To Be" can be a main verb in one sentence and a helping verb in another sentence. (See "Helping Verbs" on page 7.)

Main verb: *Len is in the police station.*

Helping verb: *Len is walking into the police station.*

Main verb: *Harriet was at her computer.*

Helping verb: *Harriet was working at her computer.*

Main verb: *Paula has been on the roof all day.*

Helping verb: *Paula has been frying eggs on the roof all day.*

LINKING VERBS LINK

What Is a Linking Verb?

A linking verb is a verb that links. It does not show action or doing. It's more like the verb "to be."

It connects the subject of the sentence to a word or phrase in the predicate. That word or phrase is called the "subject complement" because it completes the subject. The subject complement oftens describes, identifies, renames, or explains the subject.

WHAT IS A PREDICATE?

A sentence can be divided into two parts: the complete subject and the complete predicate. The complete subject is the subject and all the words that go with it. The complete predicate contains the verb and everything in the sentence that's not part of the complete subject.

COMPLETE SUBJECT
My rich old uncle Oliver from London

COMPLETE PREDICATE
seems very jovial at home in his mansion.

The sentence all boils down to *Uncle Oliver seems jovial.*

The subject complement in the sentence above is a predicate adjective. (See "Predicate Nouns and Predicate Adjectives" below.)

List of Linking Verbs

to act	to feel	to prove	to sound
to appear	to get	to remain	to stay
to be	to grow	to seem	to taste
to become	to look	to smell	to turn

Did you notice that five linking verbs relate to the senses (to feel, to look, to smell, to taste, to sound)?

Predicate Nouns and Predicate Adjectives

"To be," the most used linking verb, and the other linking verbs can connect the **subject** to a **noun** (called the predicate noun):

Her uncle George is the world's fastest whittler.

"To be" and the other linking verbs can link the **subject** to an **adjective** (called the predicate adjective):

|Subject| | Verb | Predicate
                                | Adjective |

My aunt Loraine will be extremely overjoyed to hear that the moose got away.

The linking verbs in the sentences below are in color. Arrows connect the subjects to predicate nouns and predicate adjectives. To help you see which are which, the <u>predicate nouns</u> are underlined in black and the <u>predicate adjectives</u> are underlined in blue.

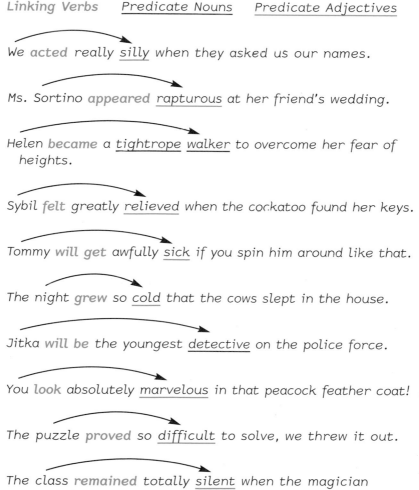

Linking Verbs   <u>Predicate Nouns</u>   <u>Predicate Adjectives</u>

We acted really <u>silly</u> when they asked us our names.

Ms. Sortino appeared <u>rapturous</u> at her friend's wedding.

Helen became a <u>tightrope walker</u> to overcome her fear of heights.

Sybil felt greatly <u>relieved</u> when the cockatoo found her keys.

Tommy will get awfully <u>sick</u> if you spin him around like that.

The night grew so <u>cold</u> that the cows slept in the house.

Jitka will be the youngest <u>detective</u> on the police force.

You look absolutely <u>marvelous</u> in that peacock feather coat!

The puzzle proved so <u>difficult</u> to solve, we threw it out.

The class remained totally <u>silent</u> when the magician sawed the teacher in half.

It *seems* <u>strange</u> to be all alone in this big castle.

Oh, that all-veggie pizza *smells* <u>delicious</u>!

Katie *sounded* so <u>happy</u> on the phone after she had won the championship.

Miriam *stayed* <u>calm</u> even though the tornado was swirling around her.

He *has been* the best loved <u>monster</u> in horror movies for many years.

Chocolate-covered beetles *taste* <u>scrumptious</u> to some people.

The boss *will turn* <u>ugly</u> if you ask her for another raise.

Linking Verbs vs. Action Verbs

Sometimes a verb that's a linking verb in one sentence can be an action or doing verb in another sentence. (Note: A verb can't be both a linking verb and an action/doing verb at the same time.)

How can you tell when a verb is a linking verb or an action/doing verb? Here's how:

Linking Verbs

If you can substitute the verb "to be" (*am, are, is, was, were, be, being, been*) for the verb and the sentence still makes sense, then the verb is a linking verb.

Consuela *became (was)* Ambassador to the Kingdom of Schlepkis in 1764.

Ashley *will feel (will be)* better after the big test is over.

Lourdes *had seemed (had been)* worried about
wallpaper that day.

Action or Doing Verbs

If you can find a direct object after the verb, then the verb is an action
verb.

> A direct object is the noun or pronoun that receives the
> action of the verb. It isn't doing anything, but some-
> thing is being done to it. Not all sentences have direct
> objects, but many do.

In the sentences below, the direct objects are underlined.

Dennis *tasted* the jellyfish <u>soup</u> only once, but that was
enough.

Lynda *could feel* the rough <u>stones</u> of Scotland with her
bare toes.

If you *smell* a <u>skunk</u>, run out the door!

Sentences with Linking and Action/Doing Verbs

Below are sentences that contain linking verbs that can also be action
or doing verbs. The same verb is used two times. The first time it's a
linking verb. The second time it's an action or doing verb.

Linking: *Mango acted young, but she was really seventy-
five in human years.*

Action: *Coco acted the part of the chicken in the
school play.*

Linking: *Sandra appeared ill after riding the roller
coaster twelve times.*

Action: *Miguel appeared in the cave unexpectedly.*

Linking: *Ms. Youngman became a teacher because she
loves kids.*

Action: *That fruity hat really becomes you.*

Linking: *Barbara felt terrific when her story was published.*

Action: *Win felt the soft rain on her nose.*

Linking: *Gerry gets giddy when we tickle him a lot.*

Action: *Judi gets gifts for us when she goes on a trip.*

Linking: *Sharmilla grew happier as she read the e-mail.*

Action: *Margaret grew potatoes in her backyard.*

Linking: *Ellen looked gorgeous in her purple wig.*

Action: *Anne looked at the purple wig and said, "That's for me!"*

Linking: *The recipe for apple pie proved easy as pie.*

Action: *The investigator proved that the piglet had done it.*

Linking: *The stew smelled pretty bad after Mr. Zalben dropped his sneaker into the pot.*

Action: *You could smell the fresh muffins as soon as you walked into Jane's house.*

Linking: *That story sounded unbelievable until Howard found out the truth.*

Action: *They sounded the burglar alarm when the mouse stole the cheese.*

Linking: *She can't stay mad at you forever, can she?*

Action: *Her cats, Smoke and Ash, can't stay home alone.*

Linking: *Fatima's three-banana sundaes taste luscious.*

Action: *If you taste this flavor, you'll never eat tutti-frutti again.*

Linking: *He turns sad when he thinks of his old school.*

Action: *Valentine always turns the key the wrong way.*

CHAPTER TWO

MORE ABOUT VERBS

VERB TENSES • REGULAR AND IRREGULAR VERBS • TRICKY VERBS • PRINCIPAL PARTS OF VERBS • ACTIVE AND PASSIVE VOICES

Past

Present

Future

VERB TENSES

What does "tense" mean?

Tense means **time**. The action expressed by a verb can be taking place right this very nanosecond (that's one billionth of a second!), or it could have already taken place a gazillion years ago, or it could be taking place a week from next Thursday.

Time is divided into three main periods:

> present
>
> past
>
> future

There are

> one **present** tense
>> —the **present** tense

> two **future** tenses
>> —the **future** tense
>>
>> —the **future perfect** tense

> three **past** tenses
>> —the **past** tense
>>
>> —the **present perfect** tense
>>
>> —the **past perfect** tense.

> That's six tenses in all.

Present Tense

The present tense shows that the action of the verb is happening right now.

> *The monkey eats the banana.*

Past Tense

The past tense shows that the action of the verb already happened at any time before right now.

> *The giraffe ate the acacia leaves.*

Future Tense

The future tense shows that the action of the verb is going to happen sometime after right now.

> *The humpback whale will eat the herring.*

Present Perfect Tense

The present perfect tense shows an action that started sometime in the past and just recently finished (or is still going on).

> *Have* or *has* is always in front of the main verb in the present perfect tense. (See "Helping Verbs" on page 7.)

The rabbit *has eaten* the carrot (and is done with it).

The rabbit *has lived* in this burrow for years (and is still living here).

Past Perfect Tense

The past perfect tense shows that an action in the past ended before another action in the past started.

> *Had* always comes before the main verb in the past perfect tense. (See "Helping Verbs" on page 7.)

The goats *had eaten* the alfalfa before the farmer knew about it.

Note that there are two past actions in that sentence: the goats eating the alfalfa and the farmer knowing about it. The eating happened before the knowing, so "*had eaten*" is in the past perfect tense.

Future Perfect Tense

The future perfect tense shows an action that will start and finish in the future.

> *Will* (or *shall*) and *have* always come before the main verb in the future perfect tense. (See "Helping Verbs" on page 7.)

The robin *will have eaten* the worms before Ms. Allen catches them.

Note that there are two future actions in that sentence: the robin eating the worms and Ms. Allen catching them. The eating will take place before the catching, so "*will have eaten*" is in the future perfect tense.

Why Are These Tenses Called "Perfect"?

One definition of "perfect" is complete, done, finished. That's the way the word is used when relating to the three perfect tenses. The present perfect tense tells us that an action is complete (*I **have caught** a fish*). The past perfect tense expresses an action that was completed before another action in the past (*I **had caught** the bus before it drove away*). The future perfect tense shows an action that will be completed before another action in the future (*I **will have caught** a cold before January ends*). So, they're the perfect tenses.

REGULAR AND IRREGULAR VERBS

All verbs in English can be divided into two categories: **regular** and **irregular.**

Regular Verbs

All you have to do to write a regular verb in the past tenses is to add *–d* or *–ed*. That's what makes a regular verb regular. (See "Verb Tenses" on page 19.) For example, in the sentences below, if you know that the present tense of "to jump" is *jump*, just add *-ed* to form the past tenses: jump + ed = jumped.

> Present tense: *Today the jolly jumpers jump from town to town.*
>
> Past tense: *Last month the jolly jumpers jumped from city to city.*
>
> Present perfect tense: *Last year the jolly jumpers had jumped from state to state.*

ADDING *-D* OR *-ED*: WHAT'S THE SPELLING RULE?

> When the last letter of the regular verb is *e*, add *–d* to spell the verb in the past tenses.
>
> Present tense: *Right now I love ice cream covered with mustard.*
>
> Past tense: *An hour ago I loved ice cream covered with ketchup.*

Present perfect tense: *For years I have loved ice cream covered with mayonnaise.*

When the last letter of the regular verb is a consonant, add *–ed* to spell the verb in the past tenses.

Present tense: *Today I look at the baby tyrannosaurus rex.*

Past tense: *Last week I looked at the baby brontosaurus.*

Present perfect tense: *For a long time I have looked at the baby stegosaurus.*

Also see "Spelling Rules When Adding *-ing* and *–ed*" on page 29.

-ED OR -T? WHICH IS RIGHT? SOMETIMES BOTH.

Some regular verbs that end with *–ed* in the past tenses can also end with *–t*. You might see them both ways, and both ways are correct.

He burned/burnt the toast for the millionth time!

Their family considers itself blessed/blest by all its fortunes.

The colors blended/blent together perfectly.

Last night Ms. Farnum dreamed/dreamt of chocolate candy bars.

For thousands of years that tribe dwelled/dwelt in these woods.

The swift gazelle leaped/leapt effortlessly over the fallen tree.

Despite his poor grades, he learned/learnt a lot at his last school.

The fried octopus in Limburger cheese smelled/smelt just awful.

Most of the thousands and thousands of verbs in English are regular. That's a relief. Regular verbs are easy. Irregular verbs aren't so easy.

Irregular Verbs

Some verbs are irregular. Irregular verbs form their past tenses in weird, unpredictable ways.

> Present tense: *Today Jeni rides her unicycle to the computer store.*
>
> Past tense: *Last week Aaron rode his bicycle to the park.*
>
> Past perfect tense: *Before that, Jessica had ridden her motorcycle to the state fair.*

When you were a little kid, you probably did what other little kids do when they are just learning English. They make all their verbs regular. You probably said sentences like

> *I eated up all my peas.*
>
> *My doggie runned around the yard.*
>
> *Mommy seed me in the show.*
>
> *Yesterday I goed to Grammy's house.*

Then, as you got older, you learned that not all verbs add *–d* or *–ed* to form their past tenses. Some verbs are irregular. So, now you say

> *I ate up all my peas.*
>
> *The dog ran around the yard.*
>
> *Mom saw me in the show.*
>
> *Yesterday I went to my grandmother's house.*

This book will show you all the common irregular verbs in English. They're the tricky ones. Luckily there are many, many more regular verbs than irregular ones.

TRICKY VERBS TO WATCH OUT FOR

Some verbs can be easily confused with other verbs, so it's a good idea to be especially careful about the verbs below.

To **awake** (to wake up from sleep) is both regular and irregular.

> *Amanda awoke (or awaked) from a deep sleep.*

To **awaken** (to wake someone up) is a regular verb.

> *They awakened Neena for school.*

To **fall** (to drop down) is an irregular verb.

He *fell* off his high horse.

To **fell** (to cut or knock down) is regular.
Dr. Sen *felled* the tree with his mighty ax.

To **hang** a picture is an irregular verb.

Lady Roslyn *hung* the Picasso in the drawing room.

To **hang** a person is a regular verb.

The cow thief *was hanged* from the highest tree.

To **lay** (to put or set down) is an irregular verb.

The hen *laid* a golden egg with silver stripes.

To **lie** (tell a falsehood) is a regular verb.

He *lied* when he said he was the king.

To **lie** (to place yourself at rest) is an irregular verb.

After dinner, Rajeev *lay* down for a nap.

To **read** sounds like "reed" in the present and future tenses and like "red" in the past tenses.

Now I'll *read* ("reed") the book that you *read* ("red") yesterday.

To **ring** (to make a bell sound) is an irregular verb.

Shana *rang* the church bell to warn the town.

To **ring** (to surround) is a regular verb.

The enemy *ringed* the town with tanks.

To **wring** (to squeeze water out of something) is an irregular verb.

Rozzie *wrung* out her bathing suit after swimming the English Channel.

To **shine** (to make shiny by rubbing) is a regular verb.

Justin *shined* his shoes until they sparkled.

To **shine** (to give off light) is both regular and irregular.

The moon *shone* (or *shined*) brightly that night.

> For more on these and other irregular verbs,
> see Full Conjugations on page 33 and
> More Irregular Verbs on page 83.

PRINCIPAL PARTS OF VERBS

What Are the Principal Parts?

There are 263 words in the conjugation of a verb. (See "What Is a Conjugation?" on page 33.) But all you have to know are three words for a verb to be able to conjugate it in twelve tenses. Those three words are called "the principal parts." "Principal" means the most important. And that's what these words are.

PRINCIPAL AND PRINCIPLE

Notice that "principal" in "principal parts" is spelled with –pal at the end, not –ple. "Principle" is a completely different word.

The Names of the Principal Parts

The principal parts of verbs have names. They are

1. Present tense: *Now you break your nose playing football.*

2. Past tense: *Last year you broke your arm playing baseball.*

3. Past participle: *Before that, you had broken your leg playing hockey.*

So, the principal parts of the verb "to break" are

PRESENT TENSE	PAST TENSE	PAST PARTICIPLE
break	broke	broken

Here's a good way to remember the principal parts of any verb. Just think of these little phrases:

Now I . . . (for the present tense)

Yesterday I . . . (for the past tense)

I have . . . (for the past participle)

PRESENT TENSE	PAST TENSE	PAST PARTICIPLE
Now I . . .	*Yesterday I . . .*	*I have . . .*
look	looked	looked
freeze	froze	frozen

The verb "to look" is regular because it ends with *–ed* in the second and third principal parts. The verb "to freeze" is irregular because it doesn't add *–d* or *–ed* in the second and third principal parts. It changes its spelling in unpredictable ways.

How to Use the Principal Parts to Form the Tenses

If you know the principal parts of a verb, you will be able to say or write the verb in all its tenses. (See "Verb Tenses" on page 19.)

Let's take the common verb "to swim." Here are its principal parts:

swim   swam   swum

The **first principal part (present tense)** is used for the **present tense:**

Today I swim in the Rappahannock River in Virginia.

and the **future tense**:

Tomorrow I will swim in the Snohomish River in Washington.

The **second principal part (past tense)** is used for the **past tense**:

> Yesterday I *swam* in the Blackstone-Woonasquatucket River in Massachusetts.

The **third principal part (past participle)** is used for the **present perfect tense**:

> I have *swum* in the Yadkin/Pee-Dee River in North Carolina four times.

and the **past perfect tense**:

> I had *swum* in the Chattahoochee River in Georgia before the Waccamaw River in South Carolina.

and the **future perfect tense**:

> I will have *swum* in the Kaskaskia River in Illinois before breakfast.

The past participle (third principal part) is also used for all six tenses in the **passive voice.** (See "Passive Voice" on page 30.)

Note: There is another principal part. It ends in *–ing*. Why isn't it here?

The other principal part is called the **present participle**. It's not included in the principal parts of verbs in this book because all you do is add *–ing* to the present tense, so it's not tricky or confusing. For example, all four principal parts of the verb "to swim" are *swim, swimming, swam, swum.*

Progressive Tenses

The present participle is used to show actions that keep on going. Because these actions are in progress and continuing, we call these forms of the verb **progressive** or **continuous**. They appear in all six tenses.

The sentences below show the progressive tenses of the verb "to stride." Its four principal parts are *stride, striding, strode, stridden.* ("To stride" means to walk with long steps.)

Present progressive tense:

> Now I *am striding* to Penrhyndeudraeth.

Past progressive tense:

Last week I was striding to Beddgelert.

Future progressive tense:

Next Monday I will be striding to Llanfairpwllgwyngyll.

Present perfect progressive tense:

For many days, I have been striding to Ynysferlas.

Past perfect progressive tense:

I had been striding to Waunfawr before I reached Hafod-y-Llyn.

Future perfect progressive tense:

I will have been striding to Aberglaslyn before I will arrive at Llanfairpwllgwyngyllgogerychwyrndrobwllllandysiliogogogoch.

Note: All the place-names above are Welsh (from Wales), and they're real!

Spelling Rules When Adding *–ing* and *–ed*

Did you notice that when *–ing* was added to "stride," the silent *e* at the end was dropped? There's a rule about that. When the verb ends with a silent *e*, **drop the *e*** before adding *–ing*.

bi**te**—biting
co**me**—coming
sli**de**—sliding

There's another spelling rule you need to know when writing verbs. When the verb ends with a single vowel (*a, e, i, o,* or *u*) followed by a single consonant, **double the consonant** before adding *–ing* or *–ed*.

bla**b**—bla**bb**ing—bla**bb**ed
pe**t**—pe**tt**ing—pe**tt**ed
chi**n**—chi**nn**ing—chi**nn**ed
ho**g**—ho**gg**ing—ho**gg**ed
dru**m**—dru**mm**ing—dru**mm**ed

ACTIVE AND PASSIVE VOICES

What Does "Voice" Mean?

Voice doesn't only mean the sound that comes out of your mouth when you speak. When referring to verbs, "voice" tells you if the subject is performing the action (**active voice**) or if the subject is doing nothing and having the action of the verb performed on him, her, or it (**passive voice**).

Active Voice

The verb is in the **active voice** when the subject of the sentence performs the action.

> The girl *hits* the ball.
>
> The girl *hit* the ball.
>
> The girl *will hit* the ball.

Passive Voice

The verb is in the **passive voice** when the subject is acted upon. The passive voice is made up of a form of the verb "to be" (*am, is, are, was, were, have been, has been, had been, will have been*) and the past participle (third principal part) of the main verb.

> The ball *is hit* by the girl.
>
> The ball *was hit* by the girl.
>
> The ball *has been hit* by the girl.

WHAT IS THE SUBJECT OF A SENTENCE?

The subject is the main person, place, thing, or idea in the sentence. The subject is what the sentence is about. The subject is the noun or pronoun that is doing the action of the verb (in the active voice) or having the action of the verb done to it (in the passive voice).

Most stories, books, newspaper reports, and magazine articles are written in the active voice (the subject performs the action) because it's more direct and forceful.

Here is a paragraph written first in the active voice, then in the passive voice, so you can see the difference.

Active Voice

He flung open the door, tossed his hat on the hook, plunked himself down in his favorite chair, grabbed his newspaper, and read the startling news that a rare bird at the zoo had built a nest out of feathers that it had plucked from a lady's hat.

Passive Voice

The door was flung open, his hat was tossed on the hook, his favorite chair was plunked in, his newspaper was grabbed, and the startling news was read by him. A nest had been built by a rare bird at the zoo out of feathers that had been plucked by it from a lady's hat.

Most people like the version with the active voice better. Why? It sounds stronger. It has more punch. It's shorter. It's livelier. Passive voice verbs sound weak to some people. That's because the subject of the sentence isn't doing anything. It's just there, having something done to it. With active voice verbs, the subject takes action.

When Is It Okay to Use the Passive Voice?

Sometimes the passive voice can be useful. You can use it to **hide the identity** of the person performing an action or if you don't know who did something.

The rule to ban gum-chewing in the school was made yesterday.

(The sentence does not reveal the name of the person who banned gum. He or she might be unpopular.)

The money for the holiday party had been lost somewhere in the gym.

(Either nobody knows who lost the money, or the speaker wants to keep the loser's name a secret.)

You can also use the passive voice to **emphasize the subject by putting it first**, even though the subject didn't do anything.

A newspaper editor may think that MAYOR IS BITTEN BY FROG (passive voice) is a better headline than FROG BITES MAYOR (active voice) because the first headline puts the most eye-catching word, *mayor,* first. The mayor didn't do anything. Something was done to the mayor, but the first word the reader sees in the headline is *mayor,* and that's what's most important. Anybody can be bitten by a frog, but when it's the mayor, that makes the headlines.

Don't Mix Active and Passive Verbs

Keep verbs in the same sentence in the same voice. Try not to mix active and passive verbs.

Not-So-Good Sentence (because the first verb is active, and the second verb is passive):

> Lorrie *studied* all night for the math test, and the highest grade *was earned* by her.

Better Sentence (both verbs are active):

> Lorrie *studied* all night for the math test and *earned* the highest grade.

Some word-processing programs that check your grammar suggest that you change all passive voice verbs to active voice verbs. You should make your own decision and use passive voice verbs when you think they express your ideas best. Just don't use them too much.

Now that you know all about regular and irregular verbs, their tenses, principal parts, voices, and how to use them, it's time to meet the 102 trickiest action-packed words in English. They're in the next two chapters.

CHAPTER THREE

FULL CONJUGATIONS
OF TWENTY-FIVE IRREGULAR VERBS

WHAT IS A CONJUGATION?

A conjugation is all the tenses of a verb, in both the active and passive voices, said or written in order: Present, Past, Future, Present Perfect, Past Perfect, Future Perfect. It is important to know the principal parts of verbs to get their conjugations right. The principal parts are shown before each conjugation below. (See "Principal Parts of Verbs" on page 26.)

SHALL AND WILL

> Some people say "I shall" and "we shall" for the future and future perfect tenses instead of "I will" and "we will." "Shall" is more British than American. Americans used to say "shall" a long time ago, but not that many people say it today. This book uses only "will," but if you hear or see "shall" in other places, that's OK, too.

How This Chapter Works

Below each tense that follows is one sentence that illustrates that whole tense. For example, let's take the verb "to bring."

PRINCIPAL PARTS		
bring	brought	brought

The **Present Perfect Tense, Passive Voice** of "to bring" is

I have been brought	we have been brought
you have been brought	you have been brought
he, she, it has been brought	they have been brought

The example sentence is

The new kids have been brought to school by a man in a giraffe suit.

But you could also say

I have been brought . . . You have been brought . . . She has been brought . . . We have been brought . . . You have been brought . . . They have been brought to school by a man in a giraffe suit.

TO BITE

PRINCIPAL PARTS		
bite	bit	bitten

PRESENT TENSE Active Voice	I bite	we bite
	you bite	you bite
	he, she, it bites	they bite

That brave little mosquito bites a lot of very big people.

PAST TENSE Active Voice	I bit	we bit
	you bit	you bit
	he, she, it bit	they bit

I chipped my front tooth when I bit into the giant nut bar.

FUTURE TENSE Active Voice	I will bite	we will bite
	you will bite	you will bite
	he, she, it will bite	they will bite

All the dogs will bite your pants if you have a hamburger in your pocket.

PRESENT PERFECT TENSE Active Voice	I have bitten	we have bitten
	you have bitten	you have bitten
	he, she, it has bitten	they have bitten

News flash: Snow White has bitten the poison apple!

PAST PERFECT TENSE Active Voice	I had bitten	we had bitten
	you had bitten	you had bitten
	he, she, it had bitten	they had bitten

She claimed that she had bitten her brother's toe by mistake.

FUTURE PERFECT TENSE Active Voice	I will have bitten	we will have bitten
	you will have bitten	you will have bitten
	he, she, it will have bitten	they will have bitten

The mice will have bitten all the cats on their tails by the end of the game.

PRESENT TENSE Passive Voice	I am bitten	we are bitten
	you are bitten	you are bitten
	he, she, it is bitten	they are bitten

Grandpa is bitten by the love bug every time he sees a cute puppy.

PAST TENSE Passive Voice	I was bitten	we were bitten
	you were bitten	you were bitten
	he, she, it was bitten	they were bitten

I think I was bitten on my nose by something, but I don't know what.

FUTURE TENSE Passive Voice	I will be bitten	we will be bitten
	you will be bitten	you will be bitten
	he, she, it will be bitten	they will be bitten

Spray a gallon of this bug repellent all over your body, or you will be bitten by a million gnats.

PRESENT PERFECT TENSE Passive Voice	I have been bitten	we have been bitten
	you have been bitten	you have been bitten
	he, she, it has been bitten	they have been bitten

The herpetologist screamed, "I have been bitten!" and dropped the rattlesnake.

PAST PERFECT TENSE Passive Voice	I had been bitten	we had been bitten
	you had been bitten	you had been bitten
	he, she, it had been bitten	they had been bitten

She fell into a deep sleep as if she had been bitten by a tsetse fly.

FUTURE PERFECT TENSE Passive Voice	I will have been bitten	we will have been bitten
	you will have been bitten	you will have been bitten
	he, she, it will have been bitten	they will have been bitten

The slow-moving beekeeper will have been bitten by all his bees by the time he puts on his protective suit.

TO BREAK

PRINCIPAL PARTS		
break	broke	broken

PRESENT TENSE Active Voice	I break	we break
	you break	you break
	he, she, it breaks	they break

That little kid breaks all the toys he plays with.

PAST TENSE Active Voice	I broke	we broke
	you broke	you broke
	he, she, it broke	they broke

She broke his heart when she said she wouldn't go on the safari with him.

FUTURE TENSE Active Voice	I will break	we will break
	you will break	you will break
	he, she, it will break	they will break

If you drop these glass flowers off the mountain, they will break.

PRESENT PERFECT TENSE Active Voice	I have broken	we have broken
	you have broken	you have broken
	he, she, it has broken	they have broken

Mom will be distressed when she finds out I have broken her statue of the elephant ballerina.

PAST PERFECT TENSE Active Voice	I had broken	we had broken
	you had broken	you had broken
	he, she, it had broken	they had broken

That year, our hockey team had broken every record in the league.

FUTURE PERFECT TENSE Active Voice	I will have broken	we will have broken
	you will have broken	you will have broken
	he, she, it will have broken	they will have broken

They will have broken the school rules if they dye their hair green.

PRESENT TENSE Passive Voice	I am broken	we are broken
	you are broken	you are broken
	he, she, it is broken	they are broken

My petunia pots are broken all the time by kids playing ball in the yard next door.

PAST TENSE Passive Voice	I was broken	we were broken
	you were broken	you were broken
	he, she, it was broken	they were broken

Honest, the window was already broken before the ball game started.

FUTURE TENSE Passive Voice	I will be broken	we will be broken
	you will be broken	you will be broken
	he, she, it will be broken	they will be broken

If you let that bull into the china shop, every plate will be broken within a few minutes.

PRESENT PERFECT TENSE Passive Voice	I have been broken	we have been broken
	you have been broken	you have been broken
	he, she, it has been broken	they have been broken

The "z" key on the keyboard has been broken, but you can still type most words without it.

PAST PERFECT TENSE Passive Voice	I had been broken	we had been broken
	you had been broken	you had been broken
	he, she, it had been broken	they had been broken

The detective noticed that the window lock had been broken.

FUTURE PERFECT TENSE Passive Voice	I will have been broken	we will have been broken
	you will have been broken	you will have been broken
	he, she, it will have been broken	they will have been broken

The wild bronco will have been broken of its bad habits before you take it home.

TO BRING

PRINCIPAL PARTS		
bring	brought	brought

PRESENT TENSE Active Voice	I bring	we bring
	you bring	you bring
	he, she, it brings	they bring

Every time Grandma visits, she brings some of her delicious fudge brownies.

PAST TENSE Active Voice	I brought	we brought
	you brought	you brought
	he, she, it brought	they brought

I brought my pet tarantula to school for show-and-tell, but my teacher made me keep it in the closet.

FUTURE TENSE Active Voice	I will bring	we will bring
	you will bring	you will bring
	he, she, it will bring	they will bring

When the message arrives, it will bring good news from the general.

PRESENT PERFECT TENSE Active Voice	I have brought	we have brought
	you have brought	you have brought
	he, she, it has brought	they have brought

The mother bird has brought many luscious worms to her babies in the nest.

PAST PERFECT TENSE Active Voice	I had brought	we had brought
	you had brought	you had brought
	he, she, it had brought	they had brought

Even with twelve suitcases, she didn't think she had brought enough clothes for the trip.

FUTURE PERFECT TENSE Active Voice	I will have brought	we will have brought
	you will have brought	you will have brought
	he, she, it will have brought	they will have brought

Mom will have brought us dry clothes by the time the rain stops.

PRESENT TENSE Passive Voice	I am brought	we are brought
	you are brought	you are brought
	he, she, it is brought	they are brought

In the jungle, the mail is brought hundreds of miles by chimpanzees.

PAST TENSE Passive Voice	I was brought	we were brought
	you were brought	you were brought
	he, she, it was brought	they were brought

These secret messages were brought out of the caves by trained bats.

FUTURE TENSE Passive Voice	I will be brought	we will be brought
	you will be brought	you will be brought
	he, she, it will be brought	they will be brought

All the kids will be brought to the party by their grandfather.

PRESENT PERFECT TENSE Passive Voice	I have been brought	we have been brought
	you have been brought	you have been brought
	he, she, it has been brought	they have been brought

We have been brought startling news by the carrier pigeon.

PAST PERFECT TENSE Passive Voice	I had been brought	we had been brought
	you had been brought	you had been brought
	he, she, it had been brought	they had been brought

The new kid had been brought to school by a man in a giraffe suit.

FUTURE PERFECT TENSE Passive Voice	I will have been brought	we will have been brought
	you will have been brought	you will have been brought
	he, she, it will have been brought	they will have been brought

The hot soup will have been brought to them by the time
they arrive at the North Pole.

TO CATCH

PRINCIPAL PARTS		
catch	caught	caught

PRESENT TENSE Active Voice	I catch	we catch
	you catch	you catch
	he, she, it catches	they catch

A Venus's-flytrap catches a lot of insects in one day.

PAST TENSE Active Voice	I caught	we caught
	you caught	you caught
	he, she, it caught	they caught

She caught the fly ball with one hand behind her back and saved the game for her team.

FUTURE TENSE Active Voice	I will catch	we will catch
	you will catch	you will catch
	he, she, it will catch	they will catch

With worms as big as snakes, you will catch fish as big as whales.

PRESENT PERFECT TENSE Active Voice	I have caught	we have caught
	you have caught	you have caught
	he, she, it has caught	they have caught

He has caught a bad cold because he played football in a snowstorm.

PAST PERFECT TENSE Active Voice	I had caught	we had caught
	you had caught	you had caught
	he, she, it had caught	they had caught

I had caught my pants on a nail, so I had to stop and sew up the hole.

FUTURE PERFECT TENSE Active Voice	I will have caught	we will have caught
	you will have caught	you will have caught
	he, she, it will have caught	they will have caught

They will have caught the last train by the time the moose has left the woods.

PRESENT TENSE Passive Voice	I am caught	we are caught
	you are caught	you are caught
	he, she, it is caught	they are caught

If you are caught with that forbidden recipe, you will not be allowed to enter your coconut pie in the contest.

PAST TENSE Passive Voice	I was caught	we were caught
	you were caught	you were caught
	he, she, it was caught	they were caught

The little fish was caught by a hook with a big worm on it.

FUTURE TENSE Passive Voice	I will be caught	we will be caught
	you will be caught	you will be caught
	he, she, it will be caught	they will be caught

The wedding bouquet will be caught by the woman who will be the next bride.

PRESENT PERFECT TENSE Passive Voice	I have been caught	we have been caught
	you have been caught	you have been caught
	he, she, it has been caught	they have been caught

The crook has been caught red-handed, stealing red gloves.

PAST PERFECT TENSE Passive Voice	I had been caught	we had been caught
	you had been caught	you had been caught
	he, she, it had been caught	they had been caught

If Tom Sawyer had been caught telling a lie, he would have been punished by Aunt Polly.

FUTURE PERFECT TENSE Passive Voice	I will have been caught	we will have been caught
	you will have been caught	you will have been caught
	he, she, it will have been caught	they will have been caught

The monkeys who escaped from the zoo will have been caught before the zoo opens.

TO CHOOSE

PRINCIPAL PARTS		
choose	chose	chosen

PRESENT TENSE Active Voice	I choose	we choose
	you choose	you choose
	he, she, it chooses	they choose

I hope they choose me to carry the grand piano up the stairs.

PAST TENSE Active Voice	I chose	we chose
	you chose	you chose
	he, she, it chose	they chose

*When he chose the small black-and-white mutt for his pet,
the dog barked happily and licked his face.*

FUTURE TENSE Active Voice	I will choose	we will choose
	you will choose	you will choose
	he, she, it will choose	they will choose

I hope, I hope, I hope she will choose me to dance with her.

PRESENT PERFECT TENSE Active Voice	I have chosen	we have chosen
	you have chosen	you have chosen
	he, she, it has chosen	they have chosen

*Grandpa has chosen the necktie with the flying hippos to
wear to his birthday party.*

PAST PERFECT TENSE Active Voice	I had chosen	we had chosen
	you had chosen	you had chosen
	he, she, it had chosen	they had chosen

*I had chosen a triple decker banana sundae with eight scoops of
ice cream and drippy caramel sauce for dessert, but my
mom said it was too messy.*

FUTURE PERFECT TENSE Active Voice	I will have chosen	we will have chosen
	you will have chosen	you will have chosen
	he, she, it will have chosen	they will have chosen

*By the time you get to the twelfth grade, you will have chosen which
colleges you want to apply to.*

PRESENT TENSE Passive Voice	I am chosen	we are chosen
	you are chosen	you are chosen
	he, she, it is chosen	they are chosen

It's a really big honor if you are chosen to ride the camel in the animal parade.

PAST TENSE Passive Voice	I was chosen	we were chosen
	you were chosen	you were chosen
	he, she, it was chosen	they were chosen

The kids in my class were chosen to greet the president when he visited my school.

FUTURE TENSE Passive Voice	I will be chosen	we will be chosen
	you will be chosen	you will be chosen
	he, she, it will be chosen	they will be chosen

You look so beautiful in your turnip costume, I am sure that you will be chosen Queen of the Vegetable Ball tonight.

PRESENT PERFECT TENSE Passive Voice	I have been chosen	we have been chosen
	you have been chosen	you have been chosen
	he, she, it has been chosen	they have been chosen

I'm so happy that I have been chosen to wrestle the alligator at the fair.

PAST PERFECT TENSE Passive Voice	I had been chosen	we had been chosen
	you had been chosen	you had been chosen
	he, she, it had been chosen	they had been chosen

That year, my turtle had been chosen "Pet of the Year" by all the kids in my neighborhood.

FUTURE PERFECT TENSE Passive Voice	I will have been chosen	we will have been chosen
	you will have been chosen	you will have been chosen
	he, she, it will have been chosen	they will have been chosen

The winner of the weirdest hat contest will have been chosen by the time we arrive at the party.

TO CUT

PRINCIPAL PARTS		
cut	cut	cut

PRESENT TENSE Active Voice	I cut	we cut
	you cut	you cut
	he, she, it cuts	they cut

If you cut up the pickles, I'll open the potato chip bags.

PAST TENSE Active Voice	I cut	we cut
	you cut	you cut
	he, she, it cut	they cut

Yesterday we cut out thousands of stars and hung them on the trees in the park.

FUTURE TENSE Active Voice	I will cut	we will cut
	you will cut	you will cut
	he, she, it will cut	they will cut

I hope the director will cut that scene out of the play because I don't want to wear the purple wig and have to sing the "Oopy Doopy" song.

PRESENT PERFECT TENSE Active Voice	I have cut	we have cut
	you have cut	you have cut
	he, she, it has cut	they have cut

The barber has cut his hair in the shape of a pineapple.

PAST PERFECT TENSE Active Voice	I had cut	we had cut
	you had cut	you had cut
	he, she, it had cut	they had cut

If they had cut out the last three speeches, the meeting would have ended on time.

FUTURE PERFECT TENSE Active Voice	I will have cut	we will have cut
	you will have cut	you will have cut
	he, she, it will have cut	they will have cut

Before we get to the party, they will have cut up all the cake and eaten it.

PRESENT TENSE Passive Voice	I am cut	we are cut
	you are cut	you are cut
	he, she, it is cut	they are cut

The pizza is cut into eight slices, but there are nine hungry kids.

PAST TENSE Passive Voice	I was cut	we were cut
	you were cut	you were cut
	he, she, it was cut	they were cut

His finger was cut, but he wasn't crying because he had fainted.

FUTURE TENSE Passive Voice	I will be cut	we will be cut
	you will be cut	you will be cut
	he, she, it will be cut	they will be cut

Don't worry, madame, your hair will be cut exactly the way you want it.

PRESENT PERFECT TENSE Passive Voice	I have been cut	we have been cut
	you have been cut	you have been cut
	he, she, it has been cut	they have been cut

He's disappointed because the picture of him being hugged by the octopus has been cut out of the yearbook.

PAST PERFECT TENSE Passive Voice	I had been cut	we had been cut
	you had been cut	you had been cut
	he, she, it had been cut	they had been cut

The daffodils had been cut too short, so they didn't fit into the vase.

FUTURE PERFECT TENSE Passive Voice	I will have been cut	we will have been cut
	you will have been cut	you will have been cut
	he, she, it will have been cut	they will have been cut

The awful "Dance of the Green Peppers" will have been cut out of the musical by the time it opens on Broadway.

45

TO DRAW

PRINCIPAL PARTS		
draw	drew	drawn

PRESENT TENSE Active Voice	I draw	we draw
	you draw	you draw
	he, she, it draws	they draw

I love the way you draw such beautiful pictures of bugs.

PAST TENSE Active Voice	I drew	we drew
	you drew	you drew
	he, she, it drew	they drew

The maid drew the curtains closed, and the prince fell fast asleep.

FUTURE TENSE Active Voice	I will draw	we will draw
	you will draw	you will draw
	he, she, it will draw	they will draw

Those six mice will draw the wagon full of duck feathers through the town.

PRESENT PERFECT TENSE Active Voice	I have drawn	we have drawn
	you have drawn	you have drawn
	he, she, it has drawn	they have drawn

I have drawn a picture of my favorite baseball star.

PAST PERFECT TENSE Active Voice	I had drawn	we had drawn
	you had drawn	you had drawn
	he, she, it had drawn	they had drawn

Before she disappeared, she had drawn the magic seeds out of her pouch.

FUTURE PERFECT TENSE Active Voice	I will have drawn	we will have drawn
	you will have drawn	you will have drawn
	he, she, it will have drawn	they will have drawn

The thirsty strangers will have drawn all the cool water from the well before anyone else has the chance to drink.

PRESENT TENSE Passive Voice	I am drawn	we are drawn
	you are drawn	you are drawn
	he, she, it is drawn	they are drawn

When the cats smell the catnip, they are drawn to the spot.

PAST TENSE Passive Voice	I was drawn	we were drawn
	you were drawn	you were drawn
	he, she, it was drawn	they were drawn

Even though all the window shades were drawn, it was still sunny in the bedroom.

FUTURE TENSE Passive Voice	I will be drawn	we will be drawn
	you will be drawn	you will be drawn
	he, she, it will be drawn	they will be drawn

The queen's portrait will be drawn by the royal painter.

PRESENT PERFECT TENSE Passive Voice	I have been drawn	we have been drawn
	you have been drawn	you have been drawn
	he, she, it has been drawn	they have been drawn

People have been drawn from all parts of the city to see the great green chicken.

PAST PERFECT TENSE Passive Voice	I had been drawn	we had been drawn
	you had been drawn	you had been drawn
	he, she, it had been drawn	they had been drawn

The dog sled had been drawn over the Siberian snow by a team of barking huskies.

FUTURE PERFECT TENSE Passive Voice	I will have been drawn	we will have been drawn
	you will have been drawn	you will have been drawn
	he, she, it will have been drawn	they will have been drawn

She will have been drawn to the mysterious fountain by the promise of eternal youth.

TO DRIVE

PRINCIPAL PARTS		
drive	drove	driven

PRESENT TENSE Active Voice	I drive	we drive
	you drive	you drive
	he, she, it drives	they drive

I'm not getting into that car if the chipmunk drives.

PAST TENSE Active Voice	I drove	we drove
	you drove	you drove
	he, she, it drove	they drove

In the story, she drove an oxcart around the world.

FUTURE TENSE Active Voice	I will drive	we will drive
	you will drive	you will drive
	he, she, it will drive	they will drive

I will drive the truck if you load the toothpicks onto the back.

PRESENT PERFECT TENSE Active Voice	I have driven	we have driven
	you have driven	you have driven
	he, she, it has driven	they have driven

That wild class has driven the poor teacher crazy.

PAST PERFECT TENSE Active Voice	I had driven	we had driven
	you had driven	you had driven
	he, she, it had driven	they had driven

The strange carpenter had driven the crystal nails deep into the hidden treasure chest.

FUTURE PERFECT TENSE Active Voice	I will have driven	we will have driven
	you will have driven	you will have driven
	he, she, it will have driven	they will have driven

You mean they will have driven all the way from Oshkosh for nothing?

PRESENT TENSE Passive Voice	I am driven	we are driven
	you are driven	you are driven
	he, she, it is driven	they are driven

The cattle are driven into their corrals by four cowgirls on white horses.

PAST TENSE Passive Voice	I was driven	we were driven
	you were driven	you were driven
	he, she, it was driven	they were driven

In those days, trains were driven by steam engines.

FUTURE TENSE Passive Voice	I will be driven	we will be driven
	you will be driven	you will be driven
	he, she, it will be driven	they will be driven

We will be driven past the castle, but we can't go in and say hi to the king.

PRESENT PERFECT TENSE Passive Voice	I have been driven	we have been driven
	you have been driven	you have been driven
	he, she, it has been driven	they have been driven

The burglar has been driven away by the ferocious barking of our pet poodle.

PAST PERFECT TENSE Passive Voice	I had been driven	we had been driven
	you had been driven	you had been driven
	he, she, it had been driven	they had been driven

He had been driven mad by the drip, drip, drip of the leaky faucet.

FUTURE PERFECT TENSE Passive Voice	I will have been driven	we will have been driven
	you will have been driven	you will have been driven
	he, she, it will have been driven	they will have been driven

The emperor will have been driven to the Fruit Ball in his apple coach.

TO FEED

PRINCIPAL PARTS		
feed	fed	fed

PRESENT TENSE Active Voice	I feed	we feed
	you feed	you feed
	he, she, it feeds	they feed

Birds feed on worms, but most people don't.

PAST TENSE Active Voice	I fed	we fed
	you fed	you fed
	he, she, it fed	they fed

What do you mean that you fed my pet mouse to my pet snake!

FUTURE TENSE Active Voice	I will feed	we will feed
	you will feed	you will feed
	he, she, it will feed	they will feed

If we go to Grandma's house, she will feed us til we burst.

PRESENT PERFECT TENSE Active Voice	I have fed	we have fed
	you have fed	you have fed
	he, she, it has fed	they have fed

The cafeteria has fed us the same sandwiches for three days in a row!

PAST PERFECT TENSE Active Voice	I had fed	we had fed
	you had fed	you had fed
	he, she, it had fed	they had fed

The babysitter had fed the children and put them to bed before the thunder boomed.

FUTURE PERFECT TENSE Active Voice	I will have fed	we will have fed
	you will have fed	you will have fed
	he, she, it will have fed	they will have fed

The farmer will have fed the pigs his own dinner by mistake before he realizes it.

PRESENT TENSE Passive Voice	I am fed	we are fed
	you are fed	you are fed
	he, she, it is fed	they are fed

The anteaters at the zoo are fed chocolate-covered ants on their birthdays.

PAST TENSE Passive Voice	I was fed	we were fed
	you were fed	you were fed
	he, she, it was fed	they were fed

It's unbelievable, but the kids at Camp Cross were fed very well.

FUTURE TENSE Passive Voice	I will be fed	we will be fed
	you will be fed	you will be fed
	he, she, it will be fed	they will be fed

At the French restaurant, you will be fed frogs' legs.

PRESENT PERFECT TENSE Passive Voice	I have been fed	we have been fed
	you have been fed	you have been fed
	he, she, it has been fed	they have been fed

I have been fed six meals a day on this cruise ship.

PAST PERFECT TENSE Passive Voice	I had been fed	we had been fed
	you had been fed	you had been fed
	he, she, it had been fed	they had been fed

The documents had been fed into the paper shredder and destroyed.

FUTURE PERFECT TENSE Passive Voice	I will have been fed	we will have been fed
	you will have been fed	you will have been fed
	he, she, it will have been fed	they will have been fed

The leftovers will have been fed to the dogs when the banquet ends.

TO FIGHT

PRINCIPAL PARTS		
fight	fought	fought

PRESENT TENSE Active Voice	I fight	we fight
	you fight	you fight
	he, she, it fights	they fight

Superheroes always fight to protect people in trouble.

PAST TENSE Active Voice	I fought	we fought
	you fought	you fought
	he, she, it fought	they fought

I fought that cold for a week with all kinds of medicines, but eventually it won.

FUTURE TENSE Active Voice	I will fight	we will fight
	you will fight	you will fight
	he, she, it will fight	they will fight

The soldiers will fight tomorrow, so they need a good night's sleep tonight.

PRESENT PERFECT TENSE Active Voice	I have fought	we have fought
	you have fought	you have fought
	he, she, it has fought	they have fought

The mayor has always fought to get the best she could for our city.

PAST PERFECT TENSE Active Voice	I had fought	we had fought
	you had fought	you had fought
	he, she, it had fought	they had fought

I had fought temptation all day, but at night I broke my diet and had pecan pie with ice cream for dessert.

FUTURE PERFECT TENSE Active Voice	I will have fought	we will have fought
	you will have fought	you will have fought
	he, she, it will have fought	they will have fought

The tyrannosauruses will have fought the brontosauruses all night.

PRESENT TENSE Passive Voice	I am fought	we are fought
	you are fought	you are fought
	he, she, it is fought	they are fought

In this war story, battles are fought on land, in the air, and on the sea.

PAST TENSE Passive Voice	I was fought	we were fought
	you were fought	you were fought
	he, she, it was fought	they were fought

Strangely, the Battle of Bunker Hill in Boston in 1775 was fought on Breed's Hill.

FUTURE TENSE Passive Voice	I will be fought	we will be fought
	you will be fought	you will be fought
	he, she, it will be fought	they will be fought

The boxing match between the kangaroo and the duck will be fought on Tuesday night.

PRESENT PERFECT TENSE Passive Voice	I have been fought	we have been fought
	you have been fought	you have been fought
	he, she, it has been fought	they have been fought

The senator has been fought on every issue she tried to bring up in Congress.

PAST PERFECT TENSE Passive Voice	I had been fought	we had been fought
	you had been fought	you had been fought
	he, she, it had been fought	they had been fought

When Rip Van Winkle woke up after twenty years, he learned that the American Revolution had been fought and won.

FUTURE PERFECT TENSE Passive Voice	I will have been fought	we will have been fought
	you will have been fought	you will have been fought
	he, she, it will have been fought	they will have been fought

The slow-moving general knows that all the major fights will have been fought by the time he reaches the battlefield.

TO FLING

PRINCIPAL PARTS		
fling	flung	flung

PRESENT TENSE Active Voice	I fling	we fling
	you fling	you fling
	he, she, it flings	they fling

Every time he flings the ball, he breaks a window.

PAST TENSE Active Voice	I flung	we flung
	you flung	you flung
	he, she, it flung	they flung

The chimps flung coconuts down on the heads of the jungle travelers.

FUTURE TENSE Active Voice	I will fling	we will fling
	you will fling	you will fling
	he, she, it will fling	they will fling

The spoiled princess will fling the dish against the wall if you serve her asparagus again.

PRESENT PERFECT TENSE Active Voice	I have flung	we have flung
	you have flung	you have flung
	he, she, it has flung	they have flung

She has flung herself into her new job with gusto.

PAST PERFECT TENSE Active Voice	I had flung	we had flung
	you had flung	you had flung
	he, she, it had flung	they had flung

They had flung caution to the wind before they boarded the hot air balloon on that windy day.

FUTURE PERFECT TENSE Active Voice	I will have flung	we will have flung
	you will have flung	you will have flung
	he, she, it will have flung	they will have flung

She will have flung a lot of weird ingredients into the pot before putting it into the oven.

PRESENT TENSE **Passive Voice**	I am flung	we are flung
	you are flung	you are flung
	he, she, it is flung	they are flung

When you ride the Monster Tornado at the carnival,
you are flung in all different directions.

PAST TENSE **Passive Voice**	I was flung	we were flung
	you were flung	you were flung
	he, she, it was flung	they were flung

The door was flung open by the violent gust of wind,
and the kitten walked in.

FUTURE TENSE **Passive Voice**	I will be flung	we will be flung
	you will be flung	you will be flung
	he, she, it will be flung	they will be flung

Lollipops will be flung from the floats in the Candyville parade.

PRESENT PERFECT TENSE **Passive Voice**	I have been flung	we have been flung
	you have been flung	you have been flung
	he, she, it has been flung	they have been flung

Huge trees have been flung around like matchsticks by the hurricane.

PAST PERFECT TENSE **Passive Voice**	I had been flung	we had been flung
	you had been flung	you had been flung
	he, she, it had been flung	they had been flung

My right shoe had been flung across the room by the furious puppy.

FUTURE PERFECT TENSE **Passive Voice**	I will have been flung	we will have been flung
	you will have been flung	you will have been flung
	he, she, it will have been flung	they will have been flung

Different meats and veggies will have been flung onto the plates
during the quickie dinner at the fast-food restaurant.

TO FORGET

PRINCIPAL PARTS		
forget	forget	forgotten/forgot

PRESENT TENSE Active Voice	I forget	we forget
	you forget	you forget
	he, she, it forgets	they forget

Then he forgets to lock the cage, so the baboon escapes.

PAST TENSE Active Voice	I forgot	we forgot
	you forgot	you forgot
	he, she, it forgot	they forgot

We completely forgot the way to our uncle's house, so we got totally lost.

FUTURE TENSE Active Voice	I will forget	we will forget
	you will forget	you will forget
	he, she, it will forget	they will forget

I guarantee that they will forget to pick up the birthday cake on the way to the party.

PRESENT PERFECT TENSE Active Voice	I have forgotten	we have forgotten
	you have forgotten	you have forgotten
	he, she, it has forgotten	they have forgotten

What do you mean you have forgotten your brother's name?

PAST PERFECT TENSE Active Voice	I had forgotten	we had forgotten
	you had forgotten	you had forgotten
	he, she, it had forgotten	they had forgotten

The princess couldn't get her crown out of the safe because she had forgotten the combination.

FUTURE PERFECT TENSE Active Voice	I will have forgotten	we will have forgotten
	you will have forgotten	you will have forgotten
	he, she, it will have forgotten	they will have forgotten

By the time we sing our song, we will have forgotten the words.

PRESENT TENSE Passive Voice	I am forgotten	we are forgotten
	you are forgotten	you are forgotten
	he, she, it is forgotten	they are forgotten

That horse used to be a famous movie star, but today it is completely forgotten.

PAST TENSE Passive Voice	I was forgotten	we were forgotten
	you were forgotten	you were forgotten
	he, she, it was forgotten	they were forgotten

The food bag was forgotten at home, so we had nothing to eat at our picnic.

FUTURE TENSE Passive Voice	I will be forgotten	we will be forgotten
	you will be forgotten	you will be forgotten
	he, she, it will be forgotten	they will be forgotten

The happy times we had at camp will never be forgotten.

PRESENT PERFECT TENSE Passive Voice	I have been forgotten	we have been forgotten
	you have been forgotten	you have been forgotten
	he, she, it has been forgotten	they have been forgotten

A lot of the heroes of the American Revolution have been forgotten.

PAST PERFECT TENSE Passive Voice	I had been forgotten	we had been forgotten
	you had been forgotten	you had been forgotten
	he, she, it had been forgotten	they had been forgotten

Those great old jokes had been forgotten until the comedian put them into his joke book.

FUTURE PERFECT TENSE Passive Voice	I will have been forgotten	we will have been forgotten
	you will have been forgotten	you will have been forgotten
	he, she, it will have been forgotten	they will have been forgotten

All the bad tricks I played on you will have been forgotten by then, and we'll be friends again, just like before.

TO FORGIVE

PRINCIPAL PARTS		
forgive	forgave	forgiven

PRESENT TENSE Active Voice	I forgive	we forgive
	you forgive	you forgive
	he, she, it forgives	they forgive

I forgive you for dropping the bricks on my toe and breaking it, but next time, please be more careful!

PAST TENSE Active Voice	I forgave	we forgave
	you forgave	you forgave
	he, she, it forgave	they forgave

Grandma forgave me for accidentally sitting on her freshly baked blueberry pie.

FUTURE TENSE Active Voice	I will forgive	we will forgive
	you will forgive	you will forgive
	he, she, it will forgive	they will forgive

I hope the teachers will forgive us for causing so much trouble on the class trip.

PRESENT PERFECT TENSE Active Voice	I have forgiven	we have forgiven
	you have forgiven	you have forgiven
	he, she, it has forgiven	they have forgiven

She has forgiven everyone who forgot to come to her party except me.

PAST PERFECT TENSE Active Voice	I had forgiven	we had forgiven
	you had forgiven	you had forgiven
	he, she, it had forgiven	they had forgiven

I thought that you had forgiven me for calling you an elephant with the brain of a flea.

FUTURE PERFECT TENSE Active Voice	I will have forgiven	we will have forgiven
	you will have forgiven	you will have forgiven
	he, she, it will have forgiven	they will have forgiven

By the time your parents hear the whole story, they will have forgiven you for flooding the basement.

PRESENT TENSE Passive Voice	I am forgiven	we are forgiven
	you are forgiven	you are forgiven
	he, she, it is forgiven	they are forgiven

You are forgiven this time for breaking the dress code, but don't wear that Frankenstein costume to school again.

PAST TENSE Passive Voice	I was forgiven	we were forgiven
	you were forgiven	you were forgiven
	he, she, it was forgiven	they were forgiven

Luckily he was forgiven for denting his mother's car, or she never would have let him drive it again.

FUTURE TENSE Passive Voice	I will be forgiven	we will be forgiven
	you will be forgiven	you will be forgiven
	he, she, it will be forgiven	they will be forgiven

If they say they're sorry enough times, they will be forgiven for what they did.

PRESENT PERFECT TENSE Passive Voice	I have been forgiven	we have been forgiven
	you have been forgiven	you have been forgiven
	he, she, it has been forgiven	they have been forgiven

Thank goodness we have been forgiven for our pranks, but we'll have to be well behaved from now on.

PAST PERFECT TENSE Passive Voice	I had been forgiven	we had been forgiven
	you had been forgiven	you had been forgiven
	he, she, it had been forgiven	they had been forgiven

You mean that even after you had been forgiven for eating all the cookies, you ate all the cake?

FUTURE PERFECT TENSE Passive Voice	I will have been forgiven	we will have been forgiven
	you will have been forgiven	you will have been forgiven
	he, she, it will have been forgiven	they will have been forgiven

By the time she finishes reading his apology, he will have been forgiven for dropping her diamond ring down the sink.

TO FREEZE

PRINCIPAL PARTS		
freeze	froze	frozen

PRESENT TENSE Active Voice	I freeze	we freeze
	you freeze	you freeze
	he, she, it freezes	they freeze

Water *freezes* when the temperature falls to 32 degrees Fahrenheit.

PAST TENSE Active Voice	I froze	we froze
	you froze	you froze
	he, she, it froze	they froze

I nearly *froze* my nose off waiting outside for you.

FUTURE TENSE Active Voice	I will freeze	we will freeze
	you will freeze	you will freeze
	he, she, it will freeze	they will freeze

You'd better wear your heavy coat, long underwear, a thick scarf, ear muffs, and two sets of gloves to the football game, or you *will freeze*.

PRESENT PERFECT TENSE Active Voice	I have frozen	we have frozen
	you have frozen	you have frozen
	he, she, it has frozen	they have frozen

I *have frozen* last night's leftovers so we can eat them again tonight.

PAST PERFECT TENSE Active Voice	I had frozen	we had frozen
	you had frozen	you had frozen
	he, she, it had frozen	they had frozen

The car lock *had frozen* solid, so Dad had to heat the key with a match to open the door.

FUTURE PERFECT TENSE Active Voice	I will have frozen	we will have frozen
	you will have frozen	you will have frozen
	he, she, it will have frozen	they will have frozen

All the beautiful flowers *will have frozen* on this frigid winter day.

PRESENT TENSE Passive Voice	I am frozen	we are frozen
	you are frozen	you are frozen
	he, she, it is frozen	they are frozen

Make sure that the ice cream bars are frozen in the refrigerated case.

PAST TENSE Passive Voice	I was frozen	we were frozen
	you were frozen	you were frozen
	he, she, it was frozen	they were frozen

The apple pies were frozen in the school freezer to keep them from spoiling until the bake sale.

FUTURE TENSE Passive Voice	I will be frozen	we will be frozen
	you will be frozen	you will be frozen
	he, she, it will be frozen	they will be frozen

If you don't pick me up at the train station on time, I will be frozen as solid as an iceberg!

PRESENT PERFECT TENSE Passive Voice	I have been frozen	we have been frozen
	you have been frozen	you have been frozen
	he, she, it has been frozen	they have been frozen

I'm sorry you think you have been frozen on purpose, but the boiler broke, and I'm trying to fix it.

PAST PERFECT TENSE Passive Voice	I had been frozen	we had been frozen
	you had been frozen	you had been frozen
	he, she, it had been frozen	they had been frozen

The trees in the park had been frozen into ice sculptures by the sudden blizzard.

FUTURE PERFECT TENSE Passive Voice	I will have been frozen	we will have been frozen
	you will have been frozen	you will have been frozen
	he, she, it will have been frozen	they will have been frozen

The audience will have been frozen solid waiting for the play to begin unless we turn on the heat.

TO GIVE

PRINCIPAL PARTS		
give	gave	given

PRESENT TENSE Active Voice	I give	we give
	you give	you give
	he, she, it gives	they give

They always *give* their all to any project they're working on.

PAST TENSE Active Voice	I gave	we gave
	you gave	you gave
	he, she, it gave	they gave

In her will, she *gave* a gazillion dollars to her favorite charity.

FUTURE TENSE Active Voice	I will give	we will give
	you will give	you will give
	he, she, it will give	they will give

I'm sure the teacher *will give* us a review before she gives us the test.

PRESENT PERFECT TENSE Active Voice	I have given	we have given
	you have given	you have given
	he, she, it has given	they have given

It *has given* me great pleasure to be your tour guide today.

PAST PERFECT TENSE Active Voice	I had given	we had given
	you had given	you had given
	he, she, it had given	they had given

The director *had given* the spoiled actress plenty of warnings before he kicked her out of the play.

FUTURE PERFECT TENSE Active Voice	I will have given	we will have given
	you will have given	you will have given
	he, she, it will have given	they will have given

He *will have given* his entire collection of ancient coins to the museum by the time he moves out of town.

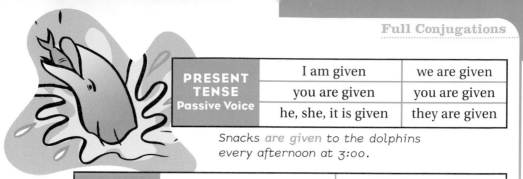

PRESENT TENSE Passive Voice	I am given	we are given
	you are given	you are given
	he, she, it is given	they are given

Snacks *are given* to the dolphins
every afternoon at 3:00.

PAST TENSE Passive Voice	I was given	we were given
	you were given	you were given
	he, she, it was given	they were given

We *were given* just a warning this time, but we'd better not do it again.

FUTURE TENSE Passive Voice	I will be given	we will be given
	you will be given	you will be given
	he, she, it will be given	they will be given

I'm sure she *will be given* the highest award for silliness
at the ceremony tonight.

PRESENT PERFECT TENSE Passive Voice	I have been given	we have been given
	you have been given	you have been given
	he, she, it has been given	they have been given

You *have been given* every possible opportunity to explain why you
wrote "Zinky Boo" on all the blackboards.

PAST PERFECT TENSE Passive Voice	I had been given	we had been given
	you had been given	you had been given
	he, she, it had been given	they had been given

After she *had been given* a million dollars by her grandfather, she
bought the school and became the principal.

FUTURE PERFECT TENSE Passive Voice	I will have been given	we will have been given
	you will have been given	you will have been given
	he, she, it will have been given	they will have been given

The speech *will have been given* before we even get to the auditorium.

TO HIDE

PRINCIPAL PARTS		
hide	hid	hidden/hid

PRESENT TENSE Active Voice	I hide	we hide
	you hide	you hide
	he, she, it hides	they hide

My cat hides its stuffed mouse behind the sofa.

PAST TENSE Active Voice	I hid	we hid
	you hid	you hid
	he, she, it hid	they hid

Her nasty little brother hid her prom gown in the freezer.

FUTURE TENSE Active Voice	I will hide	we will hide
	you will hide	you will hide
	he, she, it will hide	they will hide

I will hide all these pretzels from you if you don't stop eating them.

PRESENT PERFECT TENSE Active Voice	I have hidden	we have hidden
	you have hidden	you have hidden
	he, she, it has hidden	they have hidden

The pirates have hidden the jewels in a box in the forest.

PAST PERFECT TENSE Active Voice	I had hidden	we had hidden
	you had hidden	you had hidden
	he, she, it had hidden	they had hidden

Her rabbit had hidden her birthday gifts in the cabbage patch.

FUTURE PERFECT TENSE Active Voice	I will have hidden	we will have hidden
	you will have hidden	you will have hidden
	he, she, it will have hidden	they will have hidden

Surely the prince will have hidden his treasures before the castle is stormed.

PRESENT TENSE Passive Voice	I am hidden	we are hidden
	you are hidden	you are hidden
	he, she, it is hidden	they are hidden

The pickle is hidden under the bed, but don't tell anyone.

PAST TENSE Passive Voice	I was hidden	we were hidden
	you were hidden	you were hidden
	he, she, it was hidden	they were hidden

The diamonds were hidden for centuries under the floorboards until we bought the house and found them.

FUTURE TENSE Passive Voice	I will be hidden	we will be hidden
	you will be hidden	you will be hidden
	he, she, it will be hidden	they will be hidden

The key will be hidden under a fake rock in the garden, so let yourself in if I'm not home.

PRESENT PERFECT TENSE Passive Voice	I have been hidden	we have been hidden
	you have been hidden	you have been hidden
	he, she, it has been hidden	they have been hidden

The map has been hidden somewhere in this room, but where?

PAST PERFECT TENSE Passive Voice	I had been hidden	we had been hidden
	you had been hidden	you had been hidden
	he, she, it had been hidden	they had been hidden

The secret codes had been hidden by the enemy until they were dug up by the squirrel.

FUTURE PERFECT TENSE Passive Voice	I will have been hidden	we will have been hidden
	you will have been hidden	you will have been hidden
	he, she, it will have been hidden	they will have been hidden

She will have been hidden by her uncle until the danger ends.

TO HOLD

PRINCIPAL PARTS		
hold	held	held

PRESENT TENSE Active Voice	I hold	we hold
	you hold	you hold
	he, she, it holds	they hold

This little piece of paper holds the key to the mysteries of the universe.

PAST TENSE Active Voice	I held	we held
	you held	you held
	he, she, it held	they held

We held each other's hands as we climbed down the steep mountainside.

FUTURE TENSE Active Voice	I will hold	we will hold
	you will hold	you will hold
	he, she, it will hold	they will hold

I will hold the edge of the curtain open so you can ride your donkey onto the stage.

PRESENT PERFECT TENSE Active Voice	I have held	we have held
	you have held	you have held
	he, she, it has held	they have held

This dam has held back the river for centuries, but today it might burst.

PAST PERFECT TENSE Active Voice	I had held	we had held
	you had held	you had held
	he, she, it had held	they had held

The soldiers had held their fire for days, but now it was time for the battle to begin.

FUTURE PERFECT TENSE Active Voice	I will have held	we will have held
	you will have held	you will have held
	he, she, it will have held	they will have held

They will have held their tongues longer than they can stand.

PRESENT TENSE Passive Voice	I am held	we are held
	you are held	you are held
	he, she, it is held	they are held

The king is held a prisoner in his own castle.

PAST TENSE Passive Voice	I was held	we were held
	you were held	you were held
	he, she, it was held	they were held

That big bully was held down by that little kid until he promised not to be bad again.

FUTURE TENSE Passive Voice	I will be held	we will be held
	you will be held	you will be held
	he, she, it will be held	they will be held

The funny bunny meeting will be held tomorrow in room 325, so please be there.

PRESENT PERFECT TENSE Passive Voice	I have been held	we have been held
	you have been held	you have been held
	he, she, it has been held	they have been held

This boa constrictor is very friendly and has been held by many children.

PAST PERFECT TENSE Passive Voice	I had been held	we had been held
	you had been held	you had been held
	he, she, it had been held	they had been held

The party had been held on the day of her birthday, but she was sick and missed it.

FUTURE PERFECT TENSE Passive Voice	I will have been held	we will have been held
	you will have been held	you will have been held
	he, she, it will have been held	they will have been held

The suspect will have been held in custody by the police until the lawyer gets there.

TO KNOW

PRINCIPAL PARTS		
know	knew	known

PRESENT TENSE Active Voice	I know	we know
	you know	you know
	he, she, it knows	they know

I know the right answer, but I'm not going to tell you.

PAST TENSE Active Voice	I knew	we knew
	you knew	you knew
	he, she, it knew	they knew

It was obvious that they knew who had done the dastardly deed.

FUTURE TENSE Active Voice	I will know	we will know
	you will know	you will know
	he, she, it will know	they will know

We will know the name of the winner in just one minute.

PRESENT PERFECT TENSE Active Voice	I have known	we have known
	you have known	you have known
	he, she, it has known	they have known

The police have known for days where the spies are hiding.

PAST PERFECT TENSE Active Voice	I had known	we had known
	you had known	you had known
	he, she, it had known	they had known

If I had known it was you, I wouldn't have poured the spaghetti sauce out the window onto your head.

FUTURE PERFECT TENSE Active Voice	I will have known	we will have known
	you will have known	you will have known
	he, she, it will have known	they will have known

You will have known your new teacher's name before school opens.

PRESENT TENSE Passive Voice	I am known	we are known
	you are known	you are known
	he, she, it is known	they are known

It is well known who put the feathers in the pumpkin pie.

PAST TENSE Passive Voice	I was known	we were known
	you were known	you were known
	he, she, it was known	they were known

The singing goat was known to millions of people because of his frequent television appearances.

FUTURE TENSE Passive Voice	I will be known	we will be known
	you will be known	you will be known
	he, she, it will be known	they will be known

When we tell our story, the truth will be known, and you will be freed.

PRESENT PERFECT TENSE Passive Voice	I have been known	we have been known
	you have been known	you have been known
	he, she, it has been known	they have been known

It has been known for years that if you sit on ice cream it melts.

PAST PERFECT TENSE Passive Voice	I had been known	we had been known
	you had been known	you had been known
	he, she, it had been known	they had been known

This magician had been known all over the world for his amazing tricks, but then he disappeared.

FUTURE PERFECT TENSE Passive Voice	I will have been known	we will have been known
	you will have been known	you will have been known
	he, she, it will have been known	they will have been known

The secrets will have been known to everyone before the news gets out.

TO SEE

PRINCIPAL PARTS		
see	saw	seen

PRESENT TENSE Active Voice	I see	we see
	you see	you see
	he, she, it sees	they see

We see that you're wearing your aunt's orange wig again.

PAST TENSE Active Voice	I saw	we saw
	you saw	you saw
	he, she, it saw	they saw

Everyone saw her slip on the banana peel.

FUTURE TENSE Active Voice	I will see	we will see
	you will see	you will see
	he, she, it will see	they will see

The doctor will see you now.

PRESENT PERFECT TENSE Active Voice	I have seen	we have seen
	you have seen	you have seen
	he, she, it has seen	they have seen

I have seen crazy stunts before, but going backward down the stairs on your head beats them all.

PAST PERFECT TENSE Active Voice	I had seen	we had seen
	you had seen	you had seen
	he, she, it had seen	they had seen

They thought they had seen the Loch Ness monster, but it was only an illusion.

FUTURE PERFECT TENSE Active Voice	I will have seen	we will have seen
	you will have seen	you will have seen
	he, she, it will have seen	they will have seen

By the time you finish the tour, you will have seen all the most important sights.

PRESENT TENSE Passive Voice	I am seen	we are seen
	you are seen	you are seen
	he, she, it is seen	they are seen

The news is seen every night at 6 P.M.

PAST TENSE Passive Voice	I was seen	we were seen
	you were seen	you were seen
	he, she, it was seen	they were seen

The mystery woman was seen sneaking around in the garden.

FUTURE TENSE Passive Voice	I will be seen	we will be seen
	you will be seen	you will be seen
	he, she, it will be seen	they will be seen

If we go on television, we will be seen by all our friends.

PRESENT PERFECT TENSE Passive Voice	I have been seen	we have been seen
	you have been seen	you have been seen
	he, she, it has been seen	they have been seen

The deer that had been eating my petunias have been seen many times by my neighbors.

PAST PERFECT TENSE Passive Voice	I had been seen	we had been seen
	you had been seen	you had been seen
	he, she, it had been seen	they had been seen

He had been seen by his baseball coach sleeping in the dugout during the game.

FUTURE PERFECT TENSE Passive Voice	I will have been seen	we will have been seen
	you will have been seen	you will have been seen
	he, she, it will have been seen	they will have been seen

These pictures will have been seen by everyone before we have a chance to explain why we're dressed like grapefruit.

TO SEEK

PRINCIPAL PARTS		
seek	sought	sought

PRESENT TENSE Active Voice	I seek	we seek
	you seek	you seek
	he, she, it seeks	they seek

"If you seek to sneak a peek at the creek," said the sheik, "you'll hear a shriek and feel weak in your physique."

PAST TENSE Active Voice	I sought	we sought
	you sought	you sought
	he, she, it sought	they sought

For many years she sought the answer to the perplexing riddle.

FUTURE TENSE Active Voice	I will seek	we will seek
	you will seek	you will seek
	he, she, it will seek	they will seek

I know that they will seek out the solution no matter how long it takes.

PRESENT PERFECT TENSE Active Voice	I have sought	we have sought
	you have sought	you have sought
	he, she, it has sought	they have sought

The monkey has sought the rubber banana all over its cage.

PAST PERFECT TENSE Active Voice	I had sought	we had sought
	you had sought	you had sought
	he, she, it had sought	they had sought

Scientists had sought the missing link without realizing it was you.

FUTURE PERFECT TENSE Active Voice	I will have sought	we will have sought
	you will have sought	you will have sought
	he, she, it will have sought	they will have sought

They will have sought the treasure in vain because only I know where it is.

PRESENT TENSE Passive Voice	I am sought	we are sought
	you are sought	you are sought
	he, she, it is sought	they are sought

This famous singer *is sought* by every opera house in the world.

PAST TENSE Passive Voice	I was sought	we were sought
	you were sought	you were sought
	he, she, it was sought	they were sought

Grandma's mystery recipe for macaroni and peanut-butter pie *was sought* by all her neighbors, but she wouldn't give it to them.

FUTURE TENSE Passive Voice	I will be sought	we will be sought
	you will be sought	you will be sought
	he, she, it will be sought	they will be sought

As soon as they find out what a great basketball player she is, she *will be sought* by every college in the country.

PRESENT PERFECT TENSE Passive Voice	I have been sought	we have been sought
	you have been sought	you have been sought
	he, she, it has been sought	they have been sought

The answer to the meaning of life *has been sought* for centuries by lots of people.

PAST PERFECT TENSE Passive Voice	I had been sought	we had been sought
	you had been sought	you had been sought
	he, she, it had been sought	they had been sought

The burglar *had been sought* by police in ten different states.

FUTURE PERFECT TENSE Passive Voice	I will have been sought	we will have been sought
	you will have been sought	you will have been sought
	he, she, it will have been sought	they will have been sought

The king's pardon *will have been sought* by the knight before his punishment is announced.

73

TO SHAKE

PRINCIPAL PARTS		
shake	shook	shaken

PRESENT TENSE Active Voice	I shake	we shake
	you shake	you shake
	he, she, it shakes	they shake

If you shake that can too much, what's inside will break.

PAST TENSE Active Voice	I shook	we shook
	you shook	you shook
	he, she, it shook	they shook

That trolley ride up the bumpy hill really shook me up.

FUTURE TENSE Active Voice	I will shake	we will shake
	you will shake	you will shake
	he, she, it will shake	they will shake

If an earthquake hits, it will shake this town up like nothing else.

PRESENT PERFECT TENSE Active Voice	I have shaken	we have shaken
	you have shaken	you have shaken
	he, she, it has shaken	they have shaken

The 7:15 train to Tuscaloosa has shaken our house every night for twenty years.

PAST PERFECT TENSE Active Voice	I had shaken	we had shaken
	you had shaken	you had shaken
	he, she, it had shaken	they had shaken

I had shaken the bottle as the label said, but the stuff still didn't pour out.

FUTURE PERFECT TENSE Active Voice	I will have shaken	we will have shaken
	you will have shaken	you will have shaken
	he, she, it will have shaken	they will have shaken

They will have shaken the president's hand twice on the trip to Washington.

PRESENT TENSE Passive Voice	I am shaken	we are shaken
	you are shaken	you are shaken
	he, she, it is shaken	they are shaken

We are shaken by the news that the ferret has escaped.

PAST TENSE Passive Voice	I was shaken	we were shaken
	you were shaken	you were shaken
	he, she, it was shaken	they were shaken

The spelunkers were shaken by the unexplained rumblings in the cave.

FUTURE TENSE Passive Voice	I will be shaken	we will be shaken
	you will be shaken	you will be shaken
	he, she, it will be shaken	they will be shaken

The donkey's tail will be shaken by thousands of people today for good luck.

PRESENT PERFECT TENSE Passive Voice	I have been shaken	we have been shaken
	you have been shaken	you have been shaken
	he, she, it has been shaken	they have been shaken

The paint cans have been thoroughly shaken; now it's time to paint.

PAST PERFECT TENSE Passive Voice	I had been shaken	we had been shaken
	you had been shaken	you had been shaken
	he, she, it had been shaken	they had been shaken

The old buildings had been shaken by the quake, but they didn't fall down.

FUTURE PERFECT TENSE Passive Voice	I will have been shaken	we will have been shaken
	you will have been shaken	you will have been shaken
	he, she, it will have been shaken	they will have been shaken

She will have been shaken by the shocking announcement, but she won't give up her quest.

TO STING

PRINCIPAL PARTS		
sting	stung	stung

PRESENT TENSE Active Voice	I sting	we sting
	you sting	you sting
	he, she, it stings	they sting

Be careful of those bees—they sting!

PAST TENSE Active Voice	I stung	we stung
	you stung	you stung
	he, she, it stung	they stung

A huge wasp stung my elbow as I was delivering the graduation speech.

FUTURE TENSE Active Voice	I will sting	we will sting
	you will sting	you will sting
	he, she, it will sting	they will sting

Hornets will sting the kids at the picnic if they don't use plenty of bug spray.

PRESENT PERFECT TENSE Active Voice	I have stung	we have stung
	you have stung	you have stung
	he, she, it has stung	they have stung

"I have stung the king!" shouted the bee triumphantly.

PAST PERFECT TENSE Active Voice	I had stung	we had stung
	you had stung	you had stung
	he, she, it had stung	they had stung

Even before that nasty little fire ant had stung me, I tried to swat it with my newspaper.

FUTURE PERFECT TENSE Active Voice	I will have stung	we will have stung
	you will have stung	you will have stung
	he, she, it will have stung	they will have stung

The angry wasps will have stung the audience at the outdoor concert before we can get the people back inside the theater.

PRESENT TENSE Passive Voice	I am stung	we are stung
	you are stung	you are stung
	he, she, it is stung	they are stung

"I am stung," cried the beekeeper before he fainted.

PAST TENSE Passive Voice	I was stung	we were stung
	you were stung	you were stung
	he, she, it was stung	they were stung

We were stung by yellow jackets and had to rush to the doctor in the middle of the outdoor pageant.

FUTURE TENSE Passive Voice	I will be stung	we will be stung
	you will be stung	you will be stung
	he, she, it will be stung	they will be stung

They will be stung by her unexpected and harsh remarks.

PRESENT PERFECT TENSE Passive Voice	I have been stung	we have been stung
	you have been stung	you have been stung
	he, she, it has been stung	they have been stung

The fire fighter's eyes have been stung by the heavy smoke pouring out of the burning building.

PAST PERFECT TENSE Passive Voice	I had been stung	we had been stung
	you had been stung	you had been stung
	he, she, it had been stung	they had been stung

I had been stung on the bottom of my foot by this little needle inside my shoe.

FUTURE PERFECT TENSE Passive Voice	I will have been stung	we will have been stung
	you will have been stung	you will have been stung
	he, she, it will have been stung	they will have been stung

They will have been stung by tiny biting flies called punkies unless they seek shelter in the cave.

TO SWING

PRINCIPAL PARTS		
swing	swung	swung

PRESENT TENSE Active Voice	I swing	we swing
	you swing	you swing
	he, she, it swings	they swing

This music really swings.

PAST TENSE Active Voice	I swung	we swung
	you swung	you swung
	he, she, it swung	they swung

I swung my foot over the railing and climbed up the wall of the barn.

FUTURE TENSE Active Voice	I will swing	we will swing
	you will swing	you will swing
	he, she, it will swing	they will swing

If the pitch is good, she will swing at it.

PRESENT PERFECT TENSE Active Voice	I have swung	we have swung
	you have swung	you have swung
	he, she, it has swung	they have swung

The car with the flat tire has swung over to the side of the road.

PAST PERFECT TENSE Active Voice	I had swung	we had swung
	you had swung	you had swung
	he, she, it had swung	they had swung

The marmosets had swung from one tree to another through the jungle.

FUTURE PERFECT TENSE Active Voice	I will have swung	we will have swung
	you will have swung	you will have swung
	he, she, it will have swung	they will have swung

The models will have swung their hips as they walked down the runway at the fashion show.

PRESENT TENSE Passive Voice	I am swung	we are swung
	you are swung	you are swung
	he, she, it is swung	they are swung

*The flowerpots are swung from ropes hanging
from trees in the garden.*

PAST TENSE Passive Voice	I was swung	we were swung
	you were swung	you were swung
	he, she, it was swung	they were swung

The bat was swung wildly, and the umpire called, "Strike three!"

FUTURE TENSE Passive Voice	I will be swung	we will be swung
	you will be swung	you will be swung
	he, she, it will be swung	they will be swung

If he dances with her, he will be swung all over the ballroom floor.

PRESENT PERFECT TENSE Passive Voice	I have been swung	we have been swung
	you have been swung	you have been swung
	he, she, it has been swung	they have been swung

*This silver disk has been swung by the famous hypnotist
in front of the eyes of many people.*

PAST PERFECT TENSE Passive Voice	I had been swung	we had been swung
	you had been swung	you had been swung
	he, she, it had been swung	they had been swung

*His grandfather's gold pocket watch had been swung
from his vest like a medal of honor.*

FUTURE PERFECT TENSE Passive Voice	I will have been swung	we will have been swung
	you will have been swung	you will have been swung
	he, she, it will have been swung	they will have been swung

*Many racquets will have been swung before this tennis
tournament is over.*

TO TEACH

PRINCIPAL PARTS		
teach	taught	taught

PRESENT TENSE Active Voice	I teach	we teach
	you teach	you teach
	he, she, it teaches	they teach

At this school they teach *gum-chewing, balloon-juggling, and writing backward.*

PAST TENSE Active Voice	I taught	we taught
	you taught	you taught
	he, she, it taught	they taught

My mother taught *me never to do that, and I don't!*

FUTURE TENSE Active Voice	I will teach	we will teach
	you will teach	you will teach
	he, she, it will teach	they will teach

I hope that this will teach *you an important lesson: Never put nine sticks of gum into your mouth at once.*

PRESENT PERFECT TENSE Active Voice	I have taught	we have taught
	you have taught	you have taught
	he, she, it has taught	they have taught

Over the years, you have taught *me many valuable lessons. Thanks.*

PAST PERFECT TENSE Active Voice	I had taught	we had taught
	you had taught	you had taught
	he, she, it had taught	they had taught

I thought you had taught *your cat not to pounce on people's beds in the middle of the night.*

FUTURE PERFECT TENSE Active Voice	I will have taught	we will have taught
	you will have taught	you will have taught
	he, she, it will have taught	they will have taught

By December, she will have taught *her parrot how to sing "Jingle Bells."*

PRESENT TENSE Passive Voice	I am taught	we are taught
	you are taught	you are taught
	he, she, it is taught	they are taught

Many popular foreign languages are taught here: Kartuli, Balgarski, Cymraeg, Xhosa, and Pig Latin.

PAST TENSE Passive Voice	I was taught	we were taught
	you were taught	you were taught
	he, she, it was taught	they were taught

These children were taught manners, so they shouldn't have burped so loudly that it woke you up, madame.

FUTURE TENSE Passive Voice	I will be taught	we will be taught
	you will be taught	you will be taught
	he, she, it will be taught	they will be taught

At the animal music school, my pet turkey will be taught how to peck out tunes on his toy piano.

PRESENT PERFECT TENSE Passive Voice	I have been taught	we have been taught
	you have been taught	you have been taught
	he, she, it has been taught	they have been taught

I am qualified for this job, sir, because I have been taught how to paint my toenails in the dark.

PAST PERFECT TENSE Passive Voice	I had been taught	we had been taught
	you had been taught	you had been taught
	he, she, it had been taught	they had been taught

She had been taught how to whistle through the space between her teeth, and now she makes a living at it.

FUTURE PERFECT TENSE Passive Voice	I will have been taught	we will have been taught
	you will have been taught	you will have been taught
	he, she, it will have been taught	they will have been taught

They will have been taught all they need to know before they fly to Antarctica.

TO BE

The verb "to be" is so special, it deserves a section all by itself, so we've saved it for last. (See more about the verb "to be" on page 12.)

The Principal Parts of the verb "to be" are the trickiest of all the verbs in this book. In the present tense, there are three different verbs: *am, are,* and *is.* In the past tense, there are two different verbs: *was* and *were.* The future tense uses *be.* The last three tenses use *been.* So, the principal parts are

TO BE	**PRINCIPAL PARTS**		
	am/ are / is / be	was / were	been

PRESENT TENSE Active Voice	I am	we are
	you are	you are
	he, she, it is	they are

They are delighted that the horse can tap dance so well.

PAST TENSE Active Voice	I was	we were
	you were	you were
	he, she, it was	they were

When the phone rang, she was on the roof fixing the chimney.

FUTURE TENSE Active Voice	I will be	we will be
	you will be	you will be
	he, she, it will be	they will be

Tomorrow we will be in Argentina feeding penguins.

PRESENT PERFECT TENSE Active Voice	I have been	we have been
	you have been	you have been
	he, she, it has been	they have been

For many years, I have been in charge of the clowns and jugglers.

PAST PERFECT TENSE Active Voice	I had been	we had been
	you had been	you had been
	he, she, it had been	they had been

You had been in the wrong costume when the show started.

FUTURE PERFECT TENSE Active Voice	I will have been	we will have been
	you will have been	you will have been
	he, she, it will have been	they will have been

They will have been asleep for hours by the time the canary stops singing.

Note: There is no passive voice for the verb "to be."

CHAPTER FOUR

MORE IRREGULAR VERBS

In this chapter you'll find hundreds of sentences that illustrate all the tenses (both active and passive) of seventy-seven common irregular verbs. Each sentence is an example of one tense. This is a shortcut method for learning a verb without having to go through each of the twelve tenses fully. That saves a lot of time and effort.

How This Chapter Works

In this chapter you'll see how just one sentence can represent a whole tense. For example, the present perfect tense, active voice of the verb "to sing" is

SINGULAR	PLURAL
I have sung	we have sung
you have sung	you have sung
he, she, it has sung	they have sung

But just a single sentence like the one below can stand for that tense.

The nightingale *has sung* nonstop all night and kept the chipmunks awake.

To see what the full tense sounds like, you can replace "the nightingale" with all the pronoun subjects.

I have sung nonstop all night . . .

You have sung nonstop all night . . .

He, she, it has sung nonstop all night . . .

We have sung nonstop all night . . .

They have sung nonstop all night . . .

Just remember that

1. The verb "to be" is very irregular, so you have to learn it separately. (See "The Verb 'To Be'" on page 82.)

2. In the **present tense**, add *–s* to say the verb with **he**, **she**, or **it** (except with the verb "to be").

SINGULAR	PLURAL
I write	we write
you write	you write
he, she, it writes	they write

3. In the **present perfect tenses** (active and passive), use the helping verb *has* + *the past participle of the main verb* with **he**, **she**, and **it**. Use *have* + *the past participle of the main verb* with all the other pronoun subjects.

SINGULAR	PLURAL
I **have** written	we **have** written
you **have** written	you **have** written
he, she, it **has** written	they **have** written

See "Principal Parts of Verbs" on page 26.

Why Knowing Correct Verbs Is Important

If you know how to use verbs correctly, especially tricky irregular verbs, your speaking and writing will improve. You won't make verb mistakes, which can sometimes be embarrassing. You'll have more confidence when you speak or put pencil to paper.

Weird or Correct? Both!

You might see some verb forms in this chapter that sound weird like, "*My teacher forbade cell phones in school,*" or "*The ogre will have stridden the river with one step.*" The verbs sound odd because you don't hear them every day, but they are one hundred percent correct. Guaranteed!

SEVENTY-SEVEN IRREGULAR VERBS

Most of the verbs in this chapter have twelve tenses (six active and six passive), but some verbs are used only in the active voice.

The sentences in this chapter don't use the present participle, the second principal part that ends with *–ing*. For more about the present participle, see "Note: There is another principal part" on page 28.

TO BEAR

PRINCIPAL PARTS		
bear	bore	borne/born*

Active Voice

Present: *Now I bear the baboon on my back.*

Past: *Yesterday I bore the baboon on my back.*

Future: *Tomorrow I will bear the baboon on my back.*

Present Perfect: *I have borne/born the baboon on my back all summer.*

Past Perfect: *I had borne/born the baboon on my back before it learned to walk.*

Future Perfect: *I will have borne/born the baboon on my back until the sun rises.*

Passive Voice

Present: *The baboon is borne/born on my back now.*

Past: *The baboon was borne/born on my back yesterday.*

Future: *The baboon will be borne/born on my back tomorrow.*

Present Perfect: *The baboon has been borne/born on my back since morning.*

Past Perfect: *The baboon had been borne/born on my back before the sun set.*

Future Perfect: *The baboon will have been borne/born on my back before noon.*

*Both words are correct. You may use either one.

TO BEAT

PRINCIPAL PARTS		
beat	beat	beaten/beat*

Active Voice

Present: *You beat the eggs today.*

Past: *You beat the rugs last week.*

Future: *You will beat your brother at chess next year.*

Present Perfect: *The waves have beaten/beat the shore all day.*

Past Perfect: *She had beaten/beat the silver into a bracelet before the toast popped up.*

Future Perfect: *You will have beaten/beat the drum all night before the neighbors complain.*

Passive Voice

Present: *The eggs are beaten/beat today.*

Past: *The rugs were beaten/beat last week.*

Future: *Your brother will be beaten/beat at chess next year.*

Present Perfect: *The shore has been beaten/beat by the waves.*

Past Perfect: *The silver had been beaten/beat into a bracelet before the toast popped.*

Future Perfect: *The drum will have been beaten/beat all night before the neighbors complain.*

*Both words are correct. You may use either one.

TO BECOME

PRINCIPAL PARTS		
become	became	become

Active Voice

Present: *He becomes frightened when he sees bugs.*

Past: *He became frightened when he saw the mouse last week.*

Future: *He will become frightened when he sees the monsters tomorrow.*

Present Perfect: *He has become frightened every time he's seen a dinosaur.*

Past Perfect: *He had become frightened even before he read Dungeon of Dracula.*

Future Perfect: *He will have become frightened before the horror movie starts.*

The verb "to become" has no passive voice.

TO BEGIN

PRINCIPAL PARTS		
begin	began	begun

Active Voice

Present: *He begins the pig race right now.*

Past: *He began the pig race at 8 A.M. yesterday.*

Future: *He will begin the pig race when the sun comes up.*

Present Perfect: *He has begun the pig race at 8:00 every morning.*

Past Perfect: *He had begun the pig race before the cow mooed.*

Future Perfect: *He will have begun the pig race before the rooster crows.*

Passive Voice

Present: *The pig race is begun now.*

Past: *The pig race was begun at 8 A.M. yesterday.*

Future: *The pig race will be begun when the sun comes up.*

Present Perfect: *The pig race has been begun at 8:00 every morning.*

Past Perfect: *The pig race had been begun before the cow mooed.*

Future Perfect: *The pig race will have been begun before the rooster crows.*

TO BLEED

PRINCIPAL PARTS		
bleed	bled	bled

Active Voice

Present: *This toy doll is so realistic, it bleeds if you scratch it.*

Past: *The dragon bled when the knight stuck a sword into its solar plexus.*

Future: *These colors will bleed if you wash them in the machine.*

Present Perfect: *His nose has bled every time he's climbed up Nosebleed Hill.*

Past Perfect: *Her heart had bled for the sick animals, so she opened an animal hospital to cure them.*

Future Perfect: *That little cut will have bled all over his new shirt before he finds a bandage.*

The verb "to bleed" as used above has no passive voice.

TO BLOW

PRINCIPAL PARTS		
blow	blew	blown

Active Voice

Present: *Today he* blows *up the Flying Fish balloon.*

Past: *Last year he* blew *up the Bouncing Buffalo balloon.*

Future: *Next Tuesday he* will blow *up the Dancing Dolphin balloon.*

Present Perfect: *He* has blown *up every Singing Snake balloon since 1972.*

Past Perfect: *He* had blown *up the Juggling Giraffe balloon before the parade began.*

Future Perfect: *He* will have blown *up the Prancing Pig balloon before the parade begins.*

Passive Voice

Present: *The Flying Fish balloon* is blown *up for every parade.*

Past: *The Bouncing Buffalo balloon* was blown *up for last year's parade.*

Future: *The Dancing Dolphin balloon* will be blown *up for next year's parade.*

Present Perfect: *The Singing Snake balloon* has been blown *up every year since 1972.*

Past Perfect: *The Juggling Giraffe balloon* had been blown *up before the parade began.*

Future Perfect: *The Prancing Pig balloon* will have been blown *up before the parade begins.*

TO BURST

PRINCIPAL PARTS		
burst	burst	burst

Active Voice

Present: *Now they* burst *the bubbles to scare the frogs.*

Past: *An hour ago they* burst *the bubbles to scare the frogs.*

Future: *An hour from now they* will burst *the bubbles to scare the frogs.*

Present Perfect: *They* have *always* burst *the bubbles to scare the frogs.*

Past Perfect: *They* had burst *the bubbles before the frogs woke up.*

Future Perfect: *They* will have burst *the bubbles before the frogs go to sleep.*

Passive Voice

Present: *Now the bubbles* are burst.

Past: *An hour ago the bubbles* were burst.

Future: *An hour from now the bubbles* will be burst.

Present Perfect: *The bubbles* have been burst *by the tricky trolls.*

Past Perfect: *The bubbles* had been burst *before the frogs woke up.*

Future Perfect: *The bubbles* will have been burst *before the frogs go to sleep.*

TO BUY

PRINCIPAL PARTS		
buy	bought	bought

Active Voice

Present: *The billionaire boy* buys *everything he wants.*

Past: *Last week the billionaire boy* bought *a computer for his dog.*

Future: *Soon the billionaire boy* will buy *the whole world.*

Present Perfect: *The billionaire boy* has bought *everything in the store.*

Past Perfect: *The billionaire boy* had bought *the castle before the king moved out.*

Future Perfect: *The billionaire boy* will have bought *the whole city before the people know it.*

Passive Voice

Present: *The "Never Makes a Spelling Mistake" pencil* is bought *by kids who can't spell.*

Past: *The "Never Falls Over" bicycle* was bought *by unbalanced people last year.*

Future: *The "Never Drips" paintbrush* will be bought *by painters who are messy.*

Present Perfect: *The "Never Gets Stuck" zipper* has been bought *for years by clothing manufacturers.*

Past Perfect: *The "Never Breaks" chalk* had been bought *before the school year began.*

Future Perfect: *The "Never Slams" door* will have been bought *before the house is built.*

TO CLING

PRINCIPAL PARTS		
cling	clung	clung

Active Voice

Present: *Now cobwebs* cling *to my clothes.*

Past: *A long time ago cobwebs* clung *to my clothes.*

Future: *Cobwebs* will cling *to your clothes if you walk into haunted houses.*

Present Perfect: *A cobweb* has clung *to my clothes for hours.*

Past Perfect: *A cobweb* had clung *to my clothes for a day until I brushed it off.*

Future Perfect: *A cobweb* will have clung *to his clothes for a long time before he notices it.*

The verb "to cling" has no passive voice.

TO COME

PRINCIPAL PARTS		
come	came	come

Active Voice

Present: *The rain* comes *just when you don't want it to.*

Past: *The blizzard* came *yesterday in the middle of the football game.*

Future: *The hurricane* will come *next week when the people are dancing.*

Present Perfect: *A tornado* has come *to town every March since 1842.*

Past Perfect: *The tsunami* had come *ashore before the whales sang their song.*

Future Perfect: *The cyclone* will have come *before the crabs crawl away.*

The verb "to come" has no passive voice.

TO COST

PRINCIPAL PARTS		
cost	cost	cost

Active Voice

Present: *Today it costs a fortune to fax a fish to Fiji.*

Past: *Yesterday it cost a fortune to fry a fruit in Freiberg.*

Future: *Tomorrow it will cost a fortune to fiddle-faddle in Finland.*

Present Perfect: *It has always cost a fortune to phone your friends in Faenza.*

Past Perfect: *It had cost a fortune to flap your flügelhorn in Fletschhorn before Friday.*

Future Perfect: *It will have cost a fortune to fluff your flamingo in Florida before they change the price.*

The verb "to cost" has no passive voice.

TO CREEP

PRINCIPAL PARTS		
creep	crept	crept

Active Voice

Present: *The Mighty Mini-Monster creeps on 104 legs.*

Past: *A few minutes ago, the Mighty Mini-Monster crept by on its way to the bathroom.*

Future: *Sometime next month the Mighty Mini-Monster will creep to the castle.*

Present Perfect: *For 1,000 years the Mighty Mini-Monster has crept through the town at midnight.*

Past Perfect : *The Mighty Mini-Monster had crept to Creepsville before the highway was built.*

Future Perfect: *The Mighty Mini-Monster will have crept to the top of the mountain before his legs get tired.*

The verb "to creep" has no passive voice.

TO DEAL

PRINCIPAL PARTS		
deal	dealt	dealt

Active Voice

Present: *Grandpa deals the cards very fast.*

Past: *Grandpa dealt the cards a few minutes ago.*

Future: *Grandpa will deal the cards in a little while.*

Present Perfect: *Grandpa has always dealt the cards very quickly.*

Past Perfect: *Grandpa had dealt cards before I was born.*

Future Perfect: *Grandpa will have dealt the cards before we sit down at the table.*

Passive Voice

Present: *The cards are dealt from the top of the deck.*

Past: *The cards were dealt by the magician last night.*

Future: *The cards will be dealt to all the kids later on.*

Present Perfect: *The cards have been dealt this way for centuries.*

Past Perfect: *The cards had been dealt before the players were named.*

Future Perfect: *The cards will have been dealt before we can change the rules.*

TO DIVE

PRINCIPAL PARTS		
dive	dived/dove*	dived

Active Voice

Present: *Now Dora dives daringly into the deep.*

Past: *Then Dora dived/dove daringly into the deep.*

Future: *Later Dora will dive daringly into the deep.*

Present Perfect: *Dora has dived daringly into the deep for days.*

Past Perfect: *Dora had dived daringly into the deep before the dodo departed.*

Future Perfect: *Dora will have dived daringly into the deep before the dingbats dance.*

*Both words are correct. You may use either one.
The verb "to dive" has no passive voice.

TO DO

PRINCIPAL PARTS		
do	did	done

Active Voice

Present: *My dentist's dog does tricks that you wouldn't believe.*

Past: *He did the job he was told to do, but afterward it had to be done over.*

Future: *My band will do three songs at the concert next spring.*

Present Perfect: *The barber has done a wonderful job weaving your purple hair into your orange beard.*

Past Perfect: *The performer had done all his bird calls before the parrot bit him.*

Future Perfect: *The chambermaid will have done the beds before the guests return to their room.*

Passive Voice

Present: *"The dirty deed is done," said Dom.*

Past: *"The dirty deed was done at dark," said Dick.*

Future: *"The dirty deed will be done at dusk," said Doug.*

Present Perfect: *"The dirty deed has been done before," said Dan.*

Past Perfect: *"The dirty deed had been done before dawn," said Don.*

Future Perfect: *"The dirty deed will have been done before sun is gone," said Dawn.*

TO DRINK

PRINCIPAL PARTS		
drink	drank	drunk

Active Voice

Present: *The baby drinks her bottle now.*

Past: *Mom drank her tea yesterday.*

Future: *Dad will drink his coffee tonight.*

Present Perfect: *Grandpa has drunk his soda already.*

Past Perfect: *Grandma had drunk her milk before she ate her cookie.*

Future Perfect: *We all will have drunk the water before the fish swims away.*

Passive Voice

Present: *The bottle is drunk by the baby now.*

Past: *The tea was drunk by Mom yesterday.*

Future: *The coffee will be drunk by Dad tonight.*

Present Perfect: *The soda has been drunk by Grandpa already.*

Past Perfect: *The milk had been drunk by Grandma before she ate her cookie.*

Future Perfect: *The water will have been drunk by all of us before the fish swims away.*

TO EAT

PRINCIPAL PARTS		
eat	ate	eaten

Active Voice

Present: *The monkey eats the banana.*

Past: *The giraffe ate the leaves before that.*

Future: *The bird will eat the juicy worm in an hour.*

Present Perfect: *The rabbit has eaten the cabbage in the garden all summer.*

Past Perfect: *The anteater had eaten the ants before the park closed.*

Future Perfect: *The elephant will have eaten all the nuts before the squirrels realize it.*

Passive Voice

Present: *The banana is eaten by the monkey.*

Past: *The leaves were eaten by the giraffe before that.*

Future: *The juicy worms will be eaten by the sparrow in an hour.*

Present Perfect: *The cabbage has been eaten by the rabbit all summer.*

Past Perfect: *The ants had been eaten before the park closed.*

Future Perfect: *All the nuts will have been eaten by the elephant before the squirrels realize it.*

TO FALL

PRINCIPAL PARTS		
fall	fell	fallen

Active Voice

Present: *Snow falls in the winter.*

Past: *Snow fell all day yesterday.*

Future: *Snow will fall by Christmas.*

Present Perfect: *Snow has fallen all day long.*

Past Perfect: *Snow had fallen for hours before they called off the game.*

Future Perfect: *Snow will have fallen before the show ends.*

The verb "to fall" has no passive voice.

TO FLEE

PRINCIPAL PARTS		
flee	fled	fled

Active Voice

Present: *These apes* flee *the jungle whenever they hear loud drums.*

Past: *The walruses* fled *the ocean when the sea serpent attacked.*

Future: *The antelope* will flee *the plains when the thunder booms.*

Present Perfect: *The prairie dogs* have fled *their holes when trucks roar over them.*

Past Perfect: *The birds* had fled *the treetops before the elephant bellowed.*

Future Perfect: *The mouse* will have fled *with the cheese before the cats come home.*

The verb "to flee" has no passive voice.

TO FLY

PRINCIPAL PARTS		
fly	flew	flown

Active Voice

Present: *Many birds fly south in the winter.*

Past: *The bat flew into its cave after the sun set.*

Future: *An eagle will fly to the highest branch of a tree.*

Present Perfect: *This tired canary has flown its last flight for today.*

Past Perfect: *The pterosaurs had flown freely before the dinosaurs were extinct.*

Future Perfect: *The swallows will have flown to Capistrano before the tourists get there.*

Passive Voice

Present: *This airplane is flown to California every day.*

Past: *The rocket was flown to Mars ten years ago.*

Future: *This championship kite will be flown in the contest tomorrow.*

Present Perfect: *That hot-air balloon has been flown around the world for decades.*

Past Perfect: *This fake spaceship had been flown in a science-fiction movie before real spaceships were built.*

Future Perfect: *This present will have been flown to my sister in Alaska a day before her birthday.*

TO FORBID

PRINCIPAL PARTS		
forbid	forbad/forbade*	forbidden/forbid*

Active Voice

Present: *Teachers forbid gum-chewing in this school.*

Past: *My grandmother forbad/forbade loud music in her house last summer.*

Future: *The police will forbid you from crossing the street against the light.*

Present Perfect: *Ushers have forbidden/forbid people from entering the concert without tickets.*

Past Perfect: *Guards had forbidden/forbid us from feeding the tigers before we took the food out.*

Future Perfect: *Our parents will have forbidden/forbid us from skydiving even before we ask.*

Passive Voice

Present: *You are forbidden from doing that dangerous deed today.*

Past: *You were forbidden from doing that dangerous deed yesterday.*

Future: *You will be forbidden from doing that dangerous deed tomorrow.*

Present Perfect: *You have been forbidden from doing that dangerous deed your whole life.*

Past Perfect: *You had been forbidden from doing that dangerous deed before they knew it was so dangerous.*

Future Perfect: *You will have been forbidden from doing that dangerous deed before you ask to do it.*

*Both words are correct. You may use either one in the active voice.

TO GET

PRINCIPAL PARTS		
get	got	gotten/got*

Active Voice

Present: *He gets the flu every summer.*

Past: *He got a cold last winter.*

Future: *He will get a cough next week.*

Present Perfect: *He has gotten/got the grippe once a year since he was four.*

Past Perfect: *He had gotten/got a rash before he realized those leaves were poison ivy.*

Future Perfect: *He will have gotten/got a stomachache before he finishes all that candy.*

Passive Voice

Present: *The mail is gotten every day at noon.*

Past: *The package was gotten from the post office yesterday.*

Future: *The broccoli will be gotten from the veggie market tomorrow.*

Present Perfect: *The same bouquet has been gotten from the flower shop every Friday since they were married.*

Past Perfect: *The snake food had been gotten from the pet store before they bought the snake.*

Future Perfect: *The secret message will have been gotten by the general before he suspects the plot.*

*Both spellings are correct. You may use either one.

TO GO

PRINCIPAL PARTS		
go	went	gone

Active Voice

Present: *The son goes to school at 8:30 every morning.*

Past: *The mother went to her office five minutes ago.*

Future: *The father will go to his job shortly.*

Present Perfect: *The daughter has gone to the store already.*

Past Perfect: *The cousin had gone to college before he turned seventeen.*

Future Perfect: *The cat will have gone out in the rain without an umbrella before we can stop her.*

*The verb "to go" has no passive voice.

TO GRIND

PRINCIPAL PARTS		
grind	ground	ground

Active Voice

Present: *They grind exotic coffee beans in this market.*

Past: *They ground wheat into flour at this mill in the 1800s.*

Future: *They will grind lenses for my eyeglasses at the optometrist's tomorrow.*

Present Perfect: *He has ground his teeth in his sleep for years.*

Past Perfect: *The organ grinder had ground a lot of music out of that old hurdy-gurdy before it broke.*

Future Perfect: *He will have ground meat for hamburgers before he finds out she's a vegetarian.*

Passive Voice

Present: *Exotic coffee beans are ground in this supermarket.*

Past: *Wheat was ground into flour at this mill in the 1800s.*

Future: *Lenses will be ground for my eyeglasses at the optometrist's tomorrow.*

Present Perfect: *His teeth have been ground down in his sleep for years.*

Past Perfect: *Music had been ground out of that old hurdy-gurdy before it broke.*

Future Perfect: *Meat will have been ground for the hamburgers before he finds out she's a vegetarian.*

TO GROW

PRINCIPAL PARTS		
grow	grew	grown

Active Voice

Present: *They grow potatoes in Idaho every day.*

Past: *They grew bananas on this plantation in the nineteenth century.*

Future: *They will grow cotton on these fields in a short time.*

Present Perfect: *They have grown apples in these orchards since his great-grandfather's time.*

Past Perfect: *We had grown tomatoes in the backyard until we built the swimming pool.*

Future Perfect: *They will have grown acres of those crops until they discover they're not edible.*

Passive Voice

Present: *Potatoes are grown in Idaho every day.*

Past: *Bananas were grown on this plantation in the nineteenth century.*

Future: *Cotton will be grown on these fields in a short time.*

Present Perfect: *Apples have been grown in these orchards since his great-grandfather's time.*

Past Perfect: *Tomatoes had been grown in our backyard until the swimming pool was built.*

Future Perfect: *Acres of those crops will have been grown until they discover they're not edible.*

TO HANG

PRINCIPAL PARTS		
hang	hung	hung

Note: There are two verbs called "to hang." The one that means to hang a person by a noose is a regular verb and ends with –ed in the past tenses. Its principal parts are *hang, hanged, hanged.* The verb "to hang" that's given below means to hang a thing up.

Active Voice

Present: *The artist hangs her painting on the museum wall.*

Past: *The washerwoman hung her laundry on the line at dawn.*

Future: *They will hang a sign on the side of the stadium for two weeks to announce the championship game.*

Present Perfect: *He has hung his award for bravery in the cabinet since 1918.*

Past Perfect: *She had hung the medal around her neck until the chimpanzee plucked it off.*

Future Perfect: *The kids will have hung their sneakers on the tree before their mom sees them.*

Passive Voice

Present: *Her painting is hung in the museum.*

Past: *The laundry was hung out at dawn.*

Future: *The sign will be hung on the side of the stadium for two weeks.*

Present Perfect: *The award for bravery has been hung in the cabinet since 1918.*

Past Perfect: *The medal had been hung around her neck before the chimpanzee grabbed it.*

Future Perfect: *My sneakers will have been hung on the tree before Mom sees them.*

TO HAVE

PRINCIPAL PARTS		
have	had	had

Active Voice

Present: *Now we have enough money for the class trip.*

Past: *We had the sandwiches in this bag just a few minutes ago.*

Future: *We will have just an hour to visit the White House.*

Present Perfect: *We have had the same tour guide for the last three years.*

Past Perfect: *We had had another tour guide before that.*

Future Perfect: *We will have had a great adventure by the time we get back.*

Passive Voice

Present: *In-line skates are had by most kids in this town today.*

Past: *A good time was had by all at the festival last month.*

Future: *Peanut butter sandwiches will be had for lunch tomorrow.*

Present Perfect: *Copies of the president's speech have been had by the reporters since morning.*

Past Perfect: *Loud arguments had been had on that issue before the vote was taken.*

Future Perfect: *Doubts will have been had by many people before you get the chance to explain your plan.*

TO HIT

PRINCIPAL PARTS		
hit	hit	hit

Active Voice

Present: *William Tell hits the apple with his arrow.*

Past: *Babe Ruth hit his sixtieth home run in 1927.*

Future: *The carpenter will hit the nail squarely on the head in a few seconds.*

Present Perfect: *She has hit the winning goal in the playoffs.*

Past Perfect: *Muhammad Ali had hit his opponent right in the nose before the referee stopped the fight.*

Future Perfect: *The missile will have hit its target before the enemy can duck.*

Passive Voice

Present: *The apple is hit by William Tell's arrow.*

Past: *The sixtieth home run was hit by Babe Ruth in 1927.*

Future: *The nail will be hit squarely on the head by the carpenter in a few seconds.*

Present Perfect: *The winning goal has been hit by her in the playoffs.*

Past Perfect: *The boxer's nose had been hit by Muhammad Ali's glove before the fight was stopped.*

Future Perfect: *The target will have been hit by the missile before the enemy can duck.*

TO HURT

PRINCIPAL PARTS		
hurt	hurt	hurt

Active Voice

Present: *You hurt my feelings when you say things like that.*

Past: *He hurt his big toe when he stubbed it last night.*

Future: *You will hurt your chances of getting elected if you make that speech tonight.*

Present Perfect: *Bad weather has hurt my business this week.*

Past Perfect: *She had hurt herself falling out of a tree before she was brought to the doctor's.*

Future Perfect: *They will have hurt the dancing piglets before they discover that the costumes are too tight.*

Passive Voice

Present: *I am hurt by your ridicule today.*

Past: *I was hurt by your mean pranks yesterday.*

Future: *The crab is running away so it will not be hurt by the volleyball players on the beach.*

Present Perfect: *I have been hurt by your pranks.*

Past Perfect: *I had been hurt many times by your behavior before I complained to the authorities.*

Future Perfect: *I will have been hurt again by his nastiness before he reforms himself.*

TO KEEP

PRINCIPAL PARTS		
keep	kept	kept

Active Voice

Present: *Sandee keeps the flag because she loves this country most.*

Past: *Jed kept his taxi cab clean and shiny all the time.*

Future: *William will keep his medals after the battle.*

Present Perfect: *General Ransom has kept his courage up even after being wounded.*

Past Perfect: *Sherman had kept his diaries up to date before he left the army.*

Future Perfect: *People will have kept records of the events before the war is over.*

Passive Voice

Present: *The money is kept in the bank.*

Past: *The erasers were kept in the supply closet all summer.*

Future: *The cookies will be kept in the cupboard after they are baked.*

Present Perfect: *The equipment has been kept in the lockers since school started.*

Past Perfect: *The uniforms had been kept in the closet before the game began.*

Future Perfect: *The score sheets will have been kept in the office before the judges get here.*

TO LAY

(to put
something
down)

PRINCIPAL PARTS		
lay	laid	laid

Active Voice

Present: *The mother tenderly lays her baby in his crib.*

Past: *The floor man laid the linoleum in the kitchen this morning.*

Future: *Jane will lay her doll on the couch when she gets tired of playing with it.*

Present Perfect: *This goose has laid a golden egg every day for a year.*

Past Perfect: *The waitress had laid the table for lunch before the guests arrived.*

Future Perfect: *The prospector will have laid a claim to the gold mine before the others discover his plans.*

Passive Voice

Present: *The baby is laid tenderly in his crib by his mother.*

Past: *The linoleum was laid on the kitchen floor this morning by the floor man.*

Future: *Jane's doll will be laid on the couch when she's tired of playing with it.*

Present Perfect: *A golden egg has been laid by this goose every day for a year.*

Past Perfect: *The table had been laid for lunch by the waitress before the guests arrived.*

Future Perfect: *A claim to the gold mine will have been laid by the prospector before the others discover his plans.*

TO LEAD

PRINCIPAL PARTS		
lead	led	led

Active Voice

Present: *This tunnel leads straight to the treasure room.*

Past: *He led us down a rickety flight of stairs to the dungeon at midnight.*

Future: *This little child will lead us out of this cave as soon as the sun rises.*

Present Perfect: *He has led the horse to water, but he can't make it drink.*

Past Perfect: *She had led the orchestra for twenty-five years before she retired.*

Future Perfect: *He will have led a discussion on the issues before they vote.*

Passive Voice

Present: *The marching band is led by a bandmaster who marches backward!*

Past: *During the war our country was led by a great president.*

Future: *He will be led to the secret door later today by a man in a turkey costume.*

Present Perfect: *The procession has been led every year by the queen and her royal chickens.*

Past Perfect: *She had been led to believe that his stories were true.*

Future Perfect: *He will have been led to safety by the time the rescuers reach that point.*

TO LEAVE

PRINCIPAL PARTS		
leave	left	left

Active Voice

Present: *She leaves for school every day at 8 A.M.*

Past: *She left her book bag on the school bus this afternoon.*

Future: *She will leave her homework on the teacher's desk after school today.*

Present Perfect: *She has left the gym to go to the locker room.*

Past Perfect: *She had left her money in the principal's office before the game.*

Future Perfect: *She will have left to go home by the time the game ends.*

Passive Voice

Present: *The diamond egg is left in the pot all the time.*

Past: *The purple shoelace was left at the dentist's office yesterday by mistake.*

Future: *Three yodeling mice will be left at the zoo in half an hour.*

Present Perfect: *A bag of feathers has been left with my cousin for safekeeping.*

Past Perfect: *Nothing had been left in the box before I emptied it.*

Future Perfect: *The coded instructions will have been left by the spy before the general falls asleep.*

TO LEND

PRINCIPAL PARTS		
lend	lent	lent

Active Voice

Present: *I lend her my pencils all the time, but she never returns them.*

Past: *She lent her brother a wig for the costume party last night.*

Future: *I'm sure that he will lend you the tractor tomorrow for show-and-tell at school.*

Present Perfect: *This bank has lent me gazillions of dollars in the past ten years.*

Past Perfect: *I had lent her my car before I found out that she couldn't drive.*

Future Perfect: *We will have lent them our galoshes by the time the rain starts.*

Passive Voice

Present: *Money is lent to people all the time by banks.*

Past: *This boat was lent to the royal navy during the great sea battle in 1885.*

Future: *A pineapple will be lent to the picnic people by my aunt, but she wants it back afterward.*

Present Perfect: *A hog has been lent by Farmer Steve to Farmer Alex as part of the deal.*

Past Perfect: *It had been lent out so many times that it finally broke.*

Future Perfect: *The tap-dancing turtles will have been lent to the producer of that show for opening night.*

TO LET

PRINCIPAL PARTS		
let	let	let

Active Voice

Present: *Now we let everyone swim in our pool.*

Past: *Last night Grandma let me stay up all night watching television.*

Future: *Soon I will let you do that if you promise to clean up afterward.*

Present Perfect: *They have let us play ball here since we formed the league.*

Past Perfect: *The clown had let her try on his rubber nose before she found out she was allergic to rubber.*

Future Perfect: *We will have let people into the house with muddy shoes before we get the mop out.*

Passive Voice

Present: *The hungry tigers are let in to eat at this time every day.*

Past: *We were let out of school early today.*

Future: *We will be let alone to do anything we want tomorrow.*

Present Perfect: *The hippos have been let out of their cages to be in the movie.*

Past Perfect: *We had been let to roam freely in the mall before we discovered we had no money.*

Future Perfect: *We will have been let in by the night watchman before he realizes it's a trick.*

TO LIE

PRINCIPAL PARTS		
lie	lay	lain

Note: There are two verbs called "to lie." One means not to tell the truth. That verb is regular and ends with –d in the past tenses. Its principal parts are *lie, lied, lied.* The verb "to lie" below means to place yourself at rest in a flat position. Do not confuse it with the verb "to lay" on page 113.

Active Voice

Present: *I lie in my bed each night thinking of what I have to do the next day.*

Past: *Last night I lay in bed thinking of today.*

Future: *Tomorrow at the fair, I will lie in the grass looking at the clouds.*

Present Perfect: *You have lain on that sofa for hours, so now get up and do your chores!*

Past Perfect: *The baby walrus had lain quietly on the ice for several minutes until her mother found her.*

Future Perfect: *The cat will have lain on its favorite pillow waiting patiently until its dinner is served.*

The verb "to lie" as used above has no passive voice.

TO LOSE

PRINCIPAL PARTS		
lose	lost	lost

Active Voice

Present: *He loses everything if it's not tied to him.*

Past: *I can't believe she lost her new gloves in the park yesterday.*

Future: *The prince will lose his heart when he dances with the princess tonight.*

Present Perfect: *Our team has lost every game since the start of the season.*

Past Perfect: *I had lost the combination to the lock before I got to the bank.*

Future Perfect: *He will have lost his interest by the time the boring movie ends.*

Passive Voice

Present: *The gorilla is lost by its trainer every time they go out for a walk.*

Past: *The tests were lost by the teacher, so we have to take them over.*

Future: *The money will be lost by the kid if we don't sew up the hole in his mitten.*

Present Perfect: *The map to the secret cave has been lost by the careless pirate.*

Past Perfect: *The pretzel had been lost by Lisa, but then it was found in her shoe.*

Future Perfect: *The sour pickles will have been lost by the deli by the time the picnic begins.*

TO PAY

PRINCIPAL PARTS		
pay	paid	paid

Active Voice

Present: *I pay all my bills in alphabetical order.*

Past: *She paid a hard penalty for her mistakes.*

Future: *I will pay you what you ask, but you must deliver the dinosaur bones by Thursday.*

Present Perfect: *I think that you have paid me too much for feeding your snake.*

Past Perfect: *We had paid for the computer, but they still kept sending us a bill.*

Future Perfect: *I will have paid a lot of money for this vacation, so I hope I have a good time in Gitchegoomie.*

Passive Voice

Present: *Right now, I am paid too little for this job, so I think I'll quit.*

Past: *Last time the rabbits helped us, they were paid in carrots.*

Future: *Don't worry; you will be paid on Monday for sure.*

Present Perfect: *Since I came here, I have been paid a dollar every time I took the goat out for a walk.*

Past Perfect: *The loan had been paid back before she fell in love with the banker.*

Future Perfect: *The singer will have been paid a million dollars before her first CD comes out.*

TO PUT

PRINCIPAL PARTS		
put	put	put

Active Voice

Present: *Auntie* puts *the cat outside every night at 9.*

Past: *I* put *the money right in this pocket this morning, and now it's gone.*

Future: *If you* will put *this costume on, you'll win first prize.*

Present Perfect: *We* have put *this question to the judge several times, but she never gives us an answer.*

Past Perfect: *They* had put *their homework in their book bags before they left for school that day.*

Future Perfect: *She* will have put *up with plenty of noise by the time the party upstairs is over.*

Passive Voice

Present: *Pepper* is put *into these shakers before the restaurant opens each day.*

Past: *The little kid* was put *to bed an hour ago, but now he's running around the kitchen.*

Future: *The magical turnip* will be put *into the enchanted laundry bag after the wizard gives the secret sign.*

Present Perfect: *All the bats and balls* have been put *onto the bus for the trip to the game.*

Past Perfect: *All the stuff* had been put *into the wrong drawers, so we couldn't find anything.*

Future Perfect: *The lions* will have been put *back into their cages before the lion tamer finds out we played with them.*

TO READ

PRINCIPAL PARTS		
read	read	read

Active Voice

Present: *He reads a book every night before he goes to bed.*

Past: *Granny read my last report card with a big smile on her face.*

Future: *My brother will read about me in the newspaper when he gets home.*

Present Perfect: *She has read all the sayings you stuck to the refrigerator several times.*

Past Perfect: *I had read the journal of his African safari before I went on one myself.*

Future Perfect: *Dad will have read the teacher's note before you have the chance to explain why you did that.*

Passive Voice

Present: *The school newspaper is read by all the students.*

Past: *The author's first book was read by only a few people when it was first published.*

Future: *My winning essay will be read by the principal on the radio!*

Present Perfect: *These beloved poems have been read to children at bedtime for over a hundred years.*

Past Perfect: *The sign had been read by thousands of people before anyone noticed the spelling mistake.*

Future Perfect: *Oh, no! My love note will have been read by my girlfriend's brother before she sees it.*

TO RID

PRINCIPAL PARTS		
rid	rid/ridded*	rid/ridded*

Active Voice

Present: *He rids his homework papers of all their mistakes by using a big eraser.*

Past: *She rid/ridded herself of all her debts by paying off her credit card bills in full last month.*

Future: *We will rid ourselves of these little crawling pests with this giant can of bug spray.*

Present Perfect: *The superhero has rid/ridded the planet of bad guys with his amazing powers.*

Past Perfect: *The student government had rid/ridded the school of all ridiculous rules before the second term began.*

Future Perfect: *The queen will have rid/ridded the kingdom of fattening foods before the king comes home from his travels.*

Passive Voice

Present: *Finally, she is rid of that barking dog that used to keep her up at night.*

Past: *He was rid of all his money troubles once he won the lottery.*

Future: *We will be rid of the flood in the basement as soon as the plumber comes.*

Present Perfect: *We have been rid of mice ever since we got that thirty-pound cat.*

Past Perfect: *I had been rid of my headache for hours; then my little brother came home with his friends.*

Future Perfect: *She will have been rid of all her old furniture by the time the new furniture is delivered.*

*Both words are correct. You may use either one in the active voice.

TO RIDE

PRINCIPAL PARTS		
ride	rode	ridden

Active Voice

Present: *My baby sister rides her tricycle all over the neighborhood.*

Past: *A guy in a leather jacket rode a noisy motorcycle into town the other day.*

Future: *Grandma will ride her unicycle in the parade next Sunday.*

Present Perfect: *Dad has ridden his exercycle every day for a month to lose weight.*

Past Perfect: *I had ridden my bicycle to the store before it closed.*

Future Perfect: *The circus monkey in the chicken costume will have ridden its monocycle before the clowns come out.*

Passive Voice

Present: *This train is ridden by thousands of commuters each day.*

Past: *The old wagon was ridden deep into the forest by the gnomes.*

Future: *This bus will be ridden by the mayor and her husband, so make sure it's polished bright.*

Present Perfect: *That magnificent float has been ridden in many parades over the past fifty years.*

Past Perfect: *The horse had been ridden in many races before it won its first trophy.*

Future Perfect: *The rickety cable car will have been ridden to the top of the mountain before the blizzard hits.*

TO RING

PRINCIPAL PARTS		
ring	rang	rung

Note: There are two verbs called "to ring." The one that means "to surround" is a regular verb and ends with *–ed* in the past tenses. Its principal parts are *ring, ringed, ringed.* The verb "to ring" that's given below means to make something like a bell give off a sound.

Active Voice

Present: *They ring the church bells every hour.*

Past: *The lord rang for the maid over an hour ago, but she never came.*

Future: *The room will ring with the laughter of happy children once the puppet show begins.*

Present Perfect: *The usher has rung the bell that signals the start of the second act.*

Past Perfect: *She had rung the fire alarm, but the fire was already out.*

Future Perfect: *They will have rung the doorbell three times before I get downstairs to open it.*

Passive Voice

Present: *Wedding bells are rung when people get married.*

Past: *The chimes were rung all over the country when peace was declared.*

Future: *The magical gongs will be rung by the sorcerers when the forests float up to the sky.*

Present Perfect: *This ancient bell has been rung once a year since the reign of King Gong.*

Past Perfect: *Warning bells had been rung to alert the troops that the chickens were charging.*

Future Perfect: *The castle bells will have been rung to tell the people that the king is approaching the town.*

TO RISE

PRINCIPAL PARTS		
rise	rose	risen

Active Voice

Present: *It dawned on him that the sun* rises *every morning.*

Past: *Sleeping Beauty* rose *from her bed when the prince kissed her.*

Future: *On this site* will rise *a magnificent skyscraper that will reach the clouds.*

Present Perfect: *Billowing smoke* has risen *from the crater ever since the volcano erupted.*

Past Perfect: *Dracula* had risen *from his coffin before the young maiden saw him.*

Future Perfect: *He* will have risen *early to fight the dragon before the other knights get up.*

The verb "to rise" as used above has no passive voice.

TO RUN

PRINCIPAL PARTS		
run	ran	run

Active Voice

Present: *This old car runs beautifully, even on rough roads.*

Past: *My little dog ran away last night, but I'm sure he'll come back.*

Future: *The machine I invented will run on a mixture of water and onion soup.*

Present Perfect: *She has run six miles just to say that she loves you.*

Past Perfect: *Mom had run all her errands before the kids got home from school.*

Future Perfect: *I will have run all over town looking for those buttons to sew on my gown before the royal ball.*

Passive Voice

Present: *The Funnyface Race is run in this place.*

Past: *The ferryboat was run between here and there for sixty-three years.*

Future: *The antivirus program will be run on all computers this evening to make sure they're clean.*

Present Perfect: *The engine has been run nonstop for a year with no breakdowns.*

Past Perfect: *The mechanical toy soldier had been run over by the truck, but it still worked.*

Future Perfect: *The villains will have been run out of town by the sheriff before the people wake up.*

TO SAY

PRINCIPAL PARTS		
say	said	said

Active Voice

Present: *It says in the newspaper that Martians landed on Earth today.*

Past: *An hour ago he said he was sorry, so what more do you want?*

Future: *In a little while, an announcement on the radio will say that the prime minister has left the country.*

Present Perfect: *The president has said many times that he will not run for reelection.*

Past Perfect: *I had said to him before he did it that he would get into trouble, and I was right.*

Future Perfect: *The kid with the big mouth will have said the answer to the riddle before anyone can figure it out.*

Passive Voice

Present: *It is said that ice is cold, but can you prove it?*

Past: *The name of the mystery woman was said softly just once that night and then never again.*

Future: *It will be said for years to come that he was the greatest juggler of duck feathers who ever lived.*

Present Perfect: *Prayers have been said in this church since it was built in A.D. 1166.*

Past Perfect: *The proverb had been said before, but it deserved repeating: Two rights don't make a wrong.*

Future Perfect: *Those shocking words will have been said by the duchess before I can shout, "It's not true!"*

TO SET

PRINCIPAL PARTS		
set	set	set

Active Voice

Present: *The sun sets today at 4:41 P.M.*

Past: *The sun set yesterday at 4:42 P.M.*

Future: *The sun will set tomorrow at 4:40 P.M.*

Present Perfect: *The sun has set every day for millions of years.*

Past Perfect: *The sun had set, so she turned on her headlights.*

Future Perfect: *The sun will have set before the train reaches Chicago.*

Passive Voice

Present: *The atomic clock is set to the exact right time.*

Past: *The priceless vase was set gently down on the table.*

Future: *The post will be set into concrete so the fence doesn't fall down.*

Present Perfect: *The star football player's broken arm has been set by the doctor.*

Past Perfect: *The time had been set for the start of the parade, but nobody remembered to bring a whistle.*

Future Perfect: *A place will have been set at the table for the king, but will he come to this peasant's hut for dinner?*

TO SHINE

PRINCIPAL PARTS		
shine	shone	shined

Note: There is another verb "to shine." It means to polish by rubbing. It is a regular verb and ends in –*ed* in the past tenses. Its principal parts are *shine, shined, shined*. The verb "to shine" that is given below means to give off light or to show outstanding talent in a particular field. Do not confuse "shone," the past tense of this verb, with "shown," the past participle of the verb "to show" (see page 132).

Active Voice

Present: *Happiness shines in her grandfather's eyes every time he hears her voice.*

Past: *The sun shone brightly yesterday, but today it may rain.*

Future: *This brass door will shine dazzlingly when I get finished polishing it.*

Present Perfect: *The Statue of Liberty's torch has shone in New York Harbor since 1886.*

Past Perfect: *The lighthouse beam had shone brilliantly for many years until the electricity was shut off.*

Future Perfect: *She will have shone at the gymnastics competition and will win the top prize.*

The verb "to shine" as used above has no passive voice.

TO SHOOT

PRINCIPAL PARTS		
shoot	shot	shot

Active Voice

Present: *My aunt shoots off great fireworks on the Fourth of July.*

Past: *A minute ago he shot me right in the nose with his water pistol.*

Future: *NASA will shoot a rocket beyond the solar system next year.*

Present Perfect: *The daredevils have shot the rapids in a tiny rubber raft!*

Past Perfect: *The teacher had shot an angry look at the boy who immediately stopped fooling around.*

Future Perfect: *My favorite player will have shot the winning basket while I am at the hot dog stand.*

Passive Voice

Present: *This medicine is shot into you today to keep you well tomorrow.*

Past: *Last night, thousands of gallons of water were shot out of the hose toward the raging fire.*

Future: *At the competition this afternoon, a golden arrow will be shot by the world's best archer.*

Present Perfect: *A cannonball has been shot from the top of the citadel toward the approaching army.*

Past Perfect: *Many loud firecrackers had been shot off before the neighbors complained.*

Future Perfect: *The lunar capsule will have been shot toward the moon before I get to the space center.*

TO SHOW

PRINCIPAL PARTS		
show	showed	shown/showed*

Active Voice

Present: *I love it when my uncle shows me the medals he won at the Olympics.*

Past: *The famous artist showed his latest paintings at the museum last month.*

Future: *If you ask Grandpa tomorrow, he will show you his prize-winning tomatoes.*

Present Perfect: *This brave girl has shown/showed us that she is ready to undertake this hazardous mission.*

Past Perfect: *The gas gauge had shown/showed that the tank was nearly empty, but he refused to stop and get gas.*

Future Perfect: *He will have shown/showed his honesty by confessing before they ask him.*

Passive Voice

Present: *This scary movie is shown only at midnight.*

Past: *The painting was shown to the millionaire two weeks ago, but he didn't want to buy it.*

Future: *The secret report will be shown to the prime minister in one hour.*

Present Perfect: *Award-winning quilts have been shown at this county fair for generations.*

Past Perfect: *The map had been shown to the bus driver, but he still got lost.*

Future Perfect: *The film will have been shown before I can buy my ticket.*

*Both words are correct. You may use either one in the active voice.

TO SHRINK

PRINCIPAL PARTS		
shrink	shrank/shrunk*	shrunk/shrunken*

Active Voice

Present: *Wool sweaters shrink if you get them wet.*

Past: *My best shirt shrank/shrunk in the wash yesterday.*

Future: *Your savings will shrink if you spend too much money.*

Present Perfect: *The coward has shrunk/shrunken from going on the dangerous assignment.*

Past Perfect: *The old apple had shrunk/shrunken into something that looked like a face.*

Future Perfect: *Your new clothes will have shrunk/shrunken by the time you get them out of the rain.*

Passive Voice

Present: *In this room, big pants are shrunk to fit smaller people.*

Past: *Our bank account was shrunk by all the bills we had to pay last week.*

Future: *The population of this town will be shrunk when all those people move out.*

Present Perfect: *My best scarf has been shrunk, but who did it?*

Past Perfect: *All the fruit had been shrunk into little shapes and then painted.*

Future Perfect: *My high opinion of you will have been shrunk by your bad behavior.*

*Both words are correct. You may use either one in the active voice.

TO SING

PRINCIPAL PARTS		
sing	sang/sung*	sung

Active Voice

Present: *The baby-sitter sings the kid to sleep every night.*

Past: *I sang/sung the national anthem at the baseball game last night.*

Future: *The chorus will sing three funny songs at the concert tonight.*

Present Perfect: *She has sung that same song so many times, I'm getting sick of it!*

Past Perfect: *My mother had sung opera before she married my father.*

Future Perfect: *My favorite singer will have sung her final song, and the farewell tour will be over.*

Passive Voice

Present: *This song is sung every night at bedtime at this camp.*

Past: *"Happy Birthday" was sung twice at the party because she didn't hear it the first time.*

Future: *The school song will be sung at the beginning of the graduation tomorrow night.*

Present Perfect: *That song has been sung at every football game since the new stadium was built.*

Past Perfect: *The other melody had been sung a few times, but nobody liked it.*

Future Perfect: *My poem will have been sung to the tune of "Three Blind Mice" before the show ends.*

*Both words are correct. You may use either one in the active voice.

TO SLAY

PRINCIPAL PARTS		
slay	slew	slain

Active Voice

Present: *Knights in shining armor* slay *dragons for a living.*

Past: *The funny comedian* slew *the audience with his hilarious jokes.*

Future: *Our army* will slay *the enemy in the battle tomorrow.*

Present Perfect: *Hooray! They* have slain *the fiercest ogre in the kingdom.*

Past Perfect: *My great-great-great-grandfather* had slain *many ferocious giants before he retired.*

Future Perfect: *The royal swordsmen* will have slain *the hideous troll by lunchtime.*

Passive Voice

Present: *Dragons* are slain *frequently in this book.*

Past: *All the monsters* were slain *on a hot summer day in A.D. 802.*

Future: *Don't worry. The grotesque gremlins* will be slain *before sunset.*

Present Perfect: *The most hideous creatures* have been slain *by the tiny girl in the blonde pigtails.*

Past Perfect: *We thought they* had all been slain, *but one was still alive.*

Future Perfect: *The fiendish fiends* will have been slain *before they can escape.*

TO SLEEP

PRINCIPAL PARTS		
sleep	slept	slept

Active Voice

Present: *Baby tigers* sleep *like kittens, but they grow up bigger.*

Past: *Last night we* slept *in a tent in the backyard until it rained.*

Future: *Mom and Dad* will sleep *in the Lincoln Bedroom when they stay overnight at the White House.*

Present Perfect: *My brother and I* have slept *right through the loudest thunderstorms on earth.*

Past Perfect: *Grandpa* had slept *in the same bed with his six brothers before they moved into a bigger house.*

Future Perfect: *By the time the sleeper train reaches California, we* will have slept *for almost 500 miles.*

The verb "to sleep" has no passive voice.

TO SLIDE

PRINCIPAL PARTS		
slide	slid	slid

Active Voice

Present: *My zany cousin slides in the mud down the hill behind his house.*

Past: *In last year's championships, Slugger Sal slid into home base and won the game for us.*

Future: *If you wait until the sale next week, prices will slide down.*

Present Perfect: *The cat has slid on that same slippery spot three days in a row.*

Past Perfect: *The secret agent had slid the microfilm under the door, but he never saw it.*

Future Perfect: *The chickens will have slid on the ice on the walkway before someone helps them into the coop.*

Passive Voice

Present: *The heavy bookcase is slid into the other room by the custodian.*

Past: *The grand piano was slid out the door and onto the truck by the burglars.*

Future: *The new refrigerator will be slid into the kitchen once the old one is taken out.*

Present Perfect: *The file cabinets have been slid from one side of the office to the other.*

Past Perfect: *The wide sofa was moved into place after it had been slid through the narrow doorway.*

Future Perfect: *Don't worry. The statue of the hippo will have been slid into the museum before the doors open.*

139

TO SPEAK

PRINCIPAL PARTS		
speak	spoke	spoken

Active Voice

Present: *That little girl speaks in such a loud voice.*

Past: *The teacher spoke to me about my science project this morning.*

Future: *The governor will speak on television tonight.*

Present Perfect: *I have spoken to my parents about letting me join a circus instead of going to school, and they said no.*

Past Perfect: *They had spoken French at home before they moved to the United States.*

Future Perfect: *I will have spoken to the director before the parts in the play are given out.*

Passive Voice

Present: *Little children are spoken to kindly here.*

Past: *Angry words were spoken at the meeting last night.*

Future: *The words of the pledge will be spoken after the flag ceremony.*

Present Perfect: *Wedding vows have been spoken in this old church since before the American Revolution.*

Past Perfect: *A lot of Dutch had been spoken in New York before new people arrived.*

Future Perfect: *Words will have been spoken, but actions will speak louder.*

TO SPIN

PRINCIPAL PARTS		
spin	spun	spun

Active Voice

Present: *The broken top* spins *in a wobbly way, but it stills lights up.*

Past: *The car* spun *out of control on the icy road during last night's storm.*

Future: *The blades of the windmill* will spin *faster when the wind blows stronger.*

Present Perfect: *That little spider* has spun *this amazingly big web in just a few hours.*

Past Perfect: *The storyteller* had spun *many fascinating tales for the kids before the campfire ended.*

Future Perfect: *The carnival ride* will have spun *to a stop before my head stops spinning.*

Passive Voice

Present: *The child* is spun *by her grandfather whenever she sees him.*

Past: *One hundred tops* were spun *at the top-spinning contest yesterday.*

Future: *If you go on that wild ride, you* will be spun *around and around until you get sick to your stomach.*

Present Perfect: *Many tall tales* have been spun *around this fire, but yours is the tallest.*

Past Perfect: *The castle was so old that thousands of spiderwebs* had been spun *in every room.*

Future Perfect: *I hope that the fishing line* will have been spun *tightly on the reel before you cast out your line.*

TO SPRING

PRINCIPAL PARTS		
spring	sprang/sprung*	sprung

Active Voice

Present: *The heavy door* springs *shut with a thud every time you touch it.*

Past: *The superhero* sprang/sprung *into action as soon as he heard the cry for help.*

Future: *The acrobat* will spring *from pole to pole during his act.*

Present Perfect: *The mouse* has sprung *himself loose from the trap while we were looking the other way.*

Past Perfect: *A brilliant thought* had sprung *into her mind, but then she forgot it.*

Future Perfect: *Many funny comments* will have sprung *from her lips by the time the party ends.*

Passive Voice

Present: *The spring* is sprung *the wrong way, so that's why the clock doesn't work.*

Past: *A new idea* was sprung *suddenly on an unexpecting world.*

Future: *He* will be sprung *free from jail next Tuesday.*

Present Perfect: *The escape artist* has been sprung *loose by ingenious trickery.*

Past Perfect: *The trap* had been sprung *by the master detective before the thief knew what was happening.*

Future Perfect: *The coil* will have been sprung *setting off the device before the bug can escape.*

*Both words are correct. You may use either one in the active voice.

TO STAND

PRINCIPAL PARTS		
stand	stood	stood

Active Voice

Present: *She stands in the doorway waiting for him to come home from school every day at this time.*

Past: *She stood on one foot for three hours and won the prize.*

Future: *This monument will stand here for a thousand years.*

Present Perfect: *He has stood over six feet tall since he was in the fourth grade.*

Past Perfect: *A statue of a flying pig had stood on this spot until they moved it to the dump.*

Future Perfect: *She will have stood in the snowstorm for a long time before the bus picks her up.*

Passive Voice

Present: *Whenever the three-legged chair falls over, it is stood upright again.*

Past: *The lamp was stood in the corner to light the way to the dining room.*

Future: *The flagpole will be stood up at the top of the tower for all to see.*

Present Perfect: *The piano has been stood up on its side so they can paint around it.*

Past Perfect: *The ice sculpture of an angry alligator had been stood on its tail before it melted.*

Future Perfect: *The dizzy giraffe will have been stood on its feet before we get to the zoo to see it.*

TO STEAL

PRINCIPAL PARTS		
steal	stole	stolen

Active Voice

Present: *The mouse that lives in the wall* steals *my cheese every time it can.*

Past: *The guy who did birdcalls through his nose* stole *the show last year.*

Future: *Be careful or that player* will steal *the ball from you in tonight's game.*

Present Perfect: *Grandpa* has stolen *another kiss from Grandma when she wasn't looking.*

Past Perfect: *My brother* had stolen *my science project before I could stop him.*

Future Perfect: *Thieves* will have stolen *the duchess's tiara before the police arrive on the scene.*

Passive Voice

Present: *I don't know why my money* is stolen *every time I leave it out on my desk.*

Past: *Third base* was stolen *without warning, and it won us the game.*

Future: *All your brilliant ideas* will be stolen *if you put them up on the Internet.*

Present Perfect: *"My pearls* have been stolen!*" shouted the princess.*

Past Perfect: *The goldfish* had been stolen *once before, but they got it back.*

Future Perfect: *The horse* will have been stolen *before the barn door is locked.*

TO STICK

PRINCIPAL PARTS		
stick	stuck	stuck

Active Voice

Present: *Babies* stick *things in their mouths that they shouldn't.*

Past: *We* stuck *the badges on our jackets and marched out to join the others.*

Future: *These thorns* will stick *you if you're not careful with the roses.*

Present Perfect: *I* have stuck *all the olives on the toothpicks.*

Past Perfect: *My friend and I* had stuck *together through good times and bad.*

Future Perfect: *They* will have stuck *the flowers in their buttonholes before the ceremony starts.*

Passive Voice

Present: *We* are stuck *in the mud. Send help!*

Past: *The marching band* was stuck *behind a slow-moving float for over an hour.*

Future: *She* will be stuck *at the airport all day if she misses her plane.*

Present Perfect: *Cutout letters* have been stuck *on the bulletin board to spell out our names.*

Past Perfect: *The math teacher* had been stuck *on one problem, but she finally figured it out.*

Future Perfect: *We* will have been stuck *at school all afternoon before someone picks us up.*

TO STINK

PRINCIPAL PARTS		
stink	stank/stunk*	stunk

Active Voice

Present: *It stinks in here!*

Past: *After the skunk ran by, the tent stank/stunk.*

Future: *This room will stink if you leave that rotten fruit on the table.*

Present Perfect: *The boys' bathroom has stunk from cheap aftershave lotion ever since the boys started to shave.*

Past Perfect: *The science room had stunk for a while after the experiment, but we opened the windows and cleared the air.*

Future Perfect: *The town dump will have stunk until the wind shifts.*

The verb "to stink" as used above has no passive voice.

*Both words are correct. You may use either one.

TO STRIDE

PRINCIPAL PARTS		
stride	strode	stridden

Active Voice

Present: *The giant strides the river with one step.*

Past: *Recently we strode along the path.*

Future: *We will stride across the stage during our big scene, and the audience will love it.*

Present Perfect: *I have stridden from here to China, and I'm not even a bit tired.*

Past Perfect: *Before he reached his goal, he had stridden past many forests, mountains, and valleys.*

Future Perfect: *We will have stridden a long way to see the guru before we ask him our questions.*

The verb "to stride" as used above has no passive voice.

TO STRIKE

PRINCIPAL PARTS		
strike	struck	struck/stricken*

Active Voice

Present: *I always strike while the iron is hot.*

Past: *She struck her elbow against the door and screamed.*

Future: *The little kid will strike you on the nose if you bother him again.*

Present Perfect: *My favorite baseball player has struck out for the third time.*

Past Perfect: *Lightning had struck the house before the fire department could get there.*

Future Perfect: *The clock will have struck 12:00 before Cinderella leaves the ball.*

Passive Voice

Present: *I am always struck by the beauty of that song.*

Past: *The keys were struck too hard and the keyboard broke.*

Future: *Fire will be struck from the flints if you hold them right.*

Present Perfect: *They have been struck in the face by soap bubbles.*

Past Perfect: *His bad behavior had been struck from his school records because he reformed himself.*

Future Perfect: *They will have been struck with fear until we explain the situation to them.*

*Both words are correct. You may use either one.

TO STRIVE	PRINCIPAL PARTS		
	strive	strove	striven/strived*

Active Voice

Present: *My teacher strives to do her best each day.*

Past: *Last night we strove to be the funniest clowns in the school circus.*

Future: *Tomorrow my sister will strive to learn how to fry an egg in cooking class.*

Present Perfect: *My class has striven/strived to raise money for homeless people.*

Past Perfect: *The police officers had striven/strived to protect the kids before they got into trouble.*

Future Perfect: *All the players on my team will have striven/strived to win the trophy before the finals end.*

The verb "to strive" has no passive voice.

*Both words are correct. You may use either one.

AND THE WINNER IS...

TO SWEAR

PRINCIPAL PARTS		
swear	swore	sworn

Active Voice

Present: *In the legend of King Arthur, the Knights of the Round Table* swear *everlasting loyalty to the king.*

Past: *I* swore *that I had gotten a stike with my first ball in the bowling tournament, but I hadn't.*

Future: *The witness* will swear *to tell the whole truth at the trial tomorrow.*

Present Perfect: *The kids in the club* have sworn *to obey all the rules.*

Past Perfect: *My friend* had sworn *that he would buy all his favorite singer's albums even before he met him.*

Future Perfect: *She* will have sworn *to try to do better in school before she sees her report card.*

The verb "to swear" as used above has no passive voice.

TO SWIM

PRINCIPAL PARTS		
swim	swam	swum

Active Voice

Present: *My dad swims twenty laps every morning before he goes to work.*

Past: *My neighbor swam in a river in France last summer.*

Future: *My friends and I will swim across the lake on Monday wearing all our clothes.*

Present Perfect: *Congratulations! You have swum the fastest mile in the history of our camp.*

Past Perfect: *That kid had swum in very cold water before he caught that bad cold.*

Future Perfect: *My sister will have swum from the shore to the raft and back before she hears the whistle.*

Passive Voice

Present: *Laps are swum by many people in this pool every morning.*

Past: *The canal was swum in record time a few days ago.*

Future: *The annual race will be swum by campers dressed in duck suits on Sunday.*

Present Perfect: *The English Channel has been swum many times from the 1920s to now.*

Past Perfect: *The water around the island had been swum only once, many years ago, by a swimmer from Italy.*

Future Perfect: *The raging river will have been swum by a man in a blue bathing suit before anyone knows it.*

TO TAKE

PRINCIPAL PARTS		
take	took	taken

Active Voice

Present: *My friend takes digital pictures and sends them to his relatives by e-mail.*

Past: *She took my hand and asked me to dance at the prom last night.*

Future: *If you will take the decorations to the party, I'll take the refreshments.*

Present Perfect: *Mom and Dad have taken the early bus to be home in time for dinner.*

Past Perfect: *Luckily they had taken shelter before the cyclone blew through the town.*

Future Perfect: *The driver will have taken a right at the corner before he realizes it should have been a left.*

Passive Voice

Present: *"Children who behave are taken to the zoo regularly," said the baby-sitter.*

Past: *Everybody's suggestions were taken seriously at the meeting last month.*

Future: *School pictures will be taken next Wednesday, so don't forget to wash your faces that day.*

Present Perfect: *The documents have been taken to a secret location by government agents.*

Past Perfect: *The equipment had been taken to the field before the game began.*

Future Perfect: *His back teeth will have been taken out before the new ones grow in.*

TO TEAR

PRINCIPAL PARTS		
tear	tore	torn

Active Voice

Present: *The magician* tears *the newspaper into little pieces, then puts them back together again.*

Past: *Blanca* tore *her skirt on the nail earlier today, but she sewed the rip closed perfectly.*

Future: *Be careful or the new counting machine* will tear *your money into shreds.*

Present Perfect: *The noted chef* has torn, *not cut, the lettuce for the salad.*

Past Perfect: *The child* had torn *the wrappings off the present before she discovered it wasn't hers.*

Future Perfect: *The ringmaster* will have torn *the two stuck clowns apart before the rescue workers show up.*

Passive Voice

Present: *I* am torn *between my love for peanut butter ice cream and my desire for frogs' leg salad.*

Past: *The picture* was torn *in two and thrown on the floor by the persnickety painter.*

Future: *These old buildings* will be torn *down next year to make room for a new school.*

Present Perfect: *The sidewalk* has been torn *up so the workers can lay the new drainpipes.*

Past Perfect: *The fruity hat* had been torn *off the woman's head at the circus by the hungry chimpanzee.*

Future Perfect: *The tents* will have been torn *apart by the windstorm by the time we tie them down.*

TO THINK

PRINCIPAL PARTS		
think	thought	thought

Active Voice

Present: *That cat thinks it's a dog and barks when strangers come in.*

Past: *He thought it would be a good idea to drop water balloons out the window, but it wasn't.*

Future: *The teacher will think about not giving us homework on Halloween night.*

Present Perfect: *My friend has thought about asking you to the school dance since he first met you.*

Past Perfect: *I had thought that winter was the best season of the year until spring came.*

Future Perfect: *Mom will have thought that you were lost before she remembers you went to the mall.*

Passive Voice

Present: *It is thought by some that there's a sea monster in Loch Ness in Scotland.*

Past: *The house was thought of as haunted just because ghosts lived there, but it wasn't.*

Future: *He will be thought of in years to come as one of the greatest croaking bullfrog trainers in history.*

Present Perfect: *The revolving spaghetti fork has been thought of as the invention of the century for decades.*

Past Perfect: *It had been thought that she would be the first to climb Mount Everest backward, but her sister beat her to the top.*

Future Perfect: *The plan will have been thought too dangerous until it works.*

TO THROW

PRINCIPAL PARTS		
throw	threw	thrown

Active Voice

Present: *The other team's pitcher* throws *the fastest balls I ever saw.*

Past: *My sister* threw *herself into the big chair and fell fast asleep after her final exams.*

Future: *Grandma* will throw *herself a gala eightieth birthday party in a few days.*

Present Perfect: *My brother* has thrown *out all my favorite comic books, and he says it was an accident.*

Past Perfect: *Luckily I ducked, because the man next door* had thrown *the horseshoe across his yard into mine.*

Future Perfect: *Sandee* will have thrown *a fit before Jed tells her he was just joking.*

Passive Voice

Present: *Baseballs* are *automatically* thrown *toward the batter by this machine.*

Past: *Lava* was thrown *high into the air by the erupting volcano just a few minutes ago.*

Future: *The student rider* will be thrown *by her horse if she isn't careful.*

Present Perfect: *All our energy* has been thrown *into getting this mural painted by tonight.*

Past Perfect: *Dark shadows* had been thrown *by the setting sun over the enchanted forest.*

Future Perfect: *Punches* will have been thrown *by the boys in the schoolyard before the teacher can stop the fight.*

TO WAKE

PRINCIPAL PARTS		
wake	waked/woke*	waked/woken*

Active Voice

Present: *His dog wakes him up every morning to go for a walk.*

Past: *The alarm clock waked/woke her up in time to dye her hair before school.*

Future: *Because there's no school today, the family will wake up a little later.*

Present Perfect: *The bear has waked/woken from his long hibernation.*

Past Perfect: *The man had waked/woken up to the danger in time to save himself.*

Future Perfect: *He will have waked/woken the sleeping tiger before he realizes what it is.*

Passive Voice

Present: *He is woken by loud drumming from the apartment above at 6:31 each morning.*

Past: *She was woken by her cat in the middle of last night because the cat wanted to snuggle.*

Future: *Dad will be woken by my brother three hours before they have to leave for the amusement park.*

Present Perfect: *The king has been woken by the sound of cannons in the distance.*

Past Perfect: *The hibernating bear had been woken by the first signs of spring after winter ended.*

Future Perfect: *The campers on the overnight will have been woken up by scary sounds and will go back to camp.*

*Both words are correct. You may use either one in the active voice.

TO WEAR

PRINCIPAL PARTS		
wear	wore	worn

Active Voice

Present: *She wears the most imaginative clothing to school each day.*

Past: *Dad wore a tuxedo and Mom wore a gown to the banquet last night.*

Future: *I will wear green lipstick from now on.*

Present Perfect: *My teacher has worn the same necktie every day for a week.*

Past Perfect: *He had worn one black shoe and one brown shoe to work until somebody told him.*

Future Perfect: *Some people will have worn the wrong school colors until they change their clothes.*

Passive Voice

Present: *A badge for bravery is worn with pride by every heroic police officer.*

Past: *This hat was worn by the First Lady on inauguration day.*

Future: *The gorilla costume will be worn by my sister in the fashion show tomorrow.*

Present Perfect: *His shoes have been worn so many times, there are holes in the bottoms.*

Past Perfect: *Those polka-dot suspenders had been worn by my grandfather just before he met my grandmother.*

Future Perfect: *Silver medals will have been worn by the generals before they are awarded gold ones.*

TO WRING

PRINCIPAL PARTS		
wring	wrung	wrung

Active Voice

Present: *The swimmers* wring *out their bathing suits after practice and hang them on the line.*

Past: *The principal* wrung *the truth out of us yesterday.*

Future: *Mom* will wring *her hands in distress when she hears the news about the chickens.*

Present Perfect: *The maid* has wrung *out the princess's wet towels after her milk bath.*

Past Perfect: *He* had wrung *out his shirt after the rainstorm, but it still dripped on the floor.*

Future Perfect: *The washing machine* will have wrung *out all the wet clothes before it shuts off.*

Passive Voice

Present: *This bathing suit* is wrung *out after every swim practice.*

Past: *The coat that you spilled orange juice on* was wrung *out and hung in the window to dry.*

Future: *All the baby's wet clothes* will be wrung *out before his bath.*

Present Perfect: *All of the wigs that had been soaking in the blonde dye* have been wrung *out, so the dancing cows can put them on now.*

Past Perfect: *My favorite shirt* had been wrung *out, but it still shrunk.*

Future Perfect: *The bitter truth* will have been wrung *out of the crooks before the police come.*

TO WRITE

PRINCIPAL PARTS		
write	wrote	written

Active Voice

Present: *The kids in the poetry class* write *beautiful poems.*

Past: *My class* wrote *to a class in Russia, and we got answers back.*

Future: *Mom and Dad* will write *to us from Florida and tell us how the weather is.*

Present Perfect: *They* have written *to the president asking for his autograph.*

Past Perfect: *Mark Twain* had written *other books before he wrote* Tom Sawyer.

Future Perfect: *They* will have written *out the words to the song on their palms before they get up to sing.*

Passive Voice

Present: *Terrific stories* are written *by the students in my class every day.*

Past: *Great plays* were written *by Shakespeare starting in the late 1500s.*

Future: *Directions* will be written *down and given to everyone who's coming to the hockey game.*

Present Perfect: *Thank you notes* have been written *to all the people who gave gifts.*

Past Perfect: *Grandma's famous recipes* had been written *down, but then they were lost.*

Future Perfect: *Instructions* will have been written *down so people will know what to do.*

Topic Index

Action verbs, 6, 7, 16-18

Active voice, 30-32

Being verbs, 6, 7

Conjugation, explanation of, 33

Direct object, 17

Doing verbs, 6, 7

Future perfect tense, 21

Future tense, 20

Helping verbs, 7-9, 10, 13

Imperative verbs, 10-12

Irregular verbs, 24

Linking verbs, 13-18
examples of, 14

Passive voice, 30-32

Past perfect tense, 21

Past tense, 20

Perfect tenses, explanation of, 22

Predicate, explanation of, 14

Predicate adjectives, 14-16

Predicate nouns, 14-16

Present perfect tense, 20

Present tense, 20

Principal parts of verbs, 26-28

Progressive tense, 28-29

Regular verbs, 22-23

Sentence, explanation of, 6
one word sentences, 10-11

Subject complement, 13-14

"To be," 12-13, 82

Tricky verbs, 24-25

Verb phrases, 9-10

Verbs

action verbs, 6, 7

being verbs, 6, 7

definition of, 5

doing verbs, 6, 7

helping verbs, 7-9, 10, 13

imperative verbs, 10-12

irregular verbs, 24

linking verbs, 13-18
examples of, 14

principal parts of verbs, 26-28

regular verbs, 22-23

tenses of, 19-22, 28-29

"to be," 12-13, 82-83

tricky verbs, 24-25

Verb tenses

explanation of, 19-22

future perfect tense, 21

future tense, 20

past perfect tense, 21

past tense, 20

perfect tenses, explanation of, 22

present perfect tense, 20

present tense, 20

progressive tense, 28-29

Voice

active voice, 30-32

explanation of, 30

passive voice, 30-32

Verb Index

am, 12, 82

are, 12, 82

ate, 99

be, 12, 82

bear, 87

beat, 88

beaten, 88

became, 89

become, 89

been, 12, 82

began, 90

begin, 90

begun, 90

being, 12

bit, 34

bite, 34

bitten, 34

bled, 91

bleed, 91

blew, 92

blow, 92

blown, 92

bore, 87

born, 87

borne, 87

bought, 94

break, 36

bring, 33, 38

broke, 36

broken, 36

brought, 33, 38

burst, 93

buy, 95

came, 95

catch, 40

caught, 40

choose, 42

chose, 42

chosen, 42

cling, 95

clung, 95

come, 95

cost, 96

creep, 96

crept, 96

cut, 44

deal, 97

dealt, 97

did, 99

dive, 98
dived, 98
do, 99
done, 99
dove, 98
drank, 100
draw, 46
drawn, 46
drew, 46
drink, 100
drive, 48
driven, 48
drove, 48
drunk, 100
eat, 101
eaten, 101
fall, 102
fallen, 102
fed, 50
feed, 50
fell, 102
fight, 52
fled, 103
flee, 103
flew, 105
fling, 54
flown, 104
flung, 54
fly, 104
forbad, 105
forbade, 105
forbid, 105
forbidden, 105
forgave, 58
forget, 56
forgive, 58
forgiven, 58
forgot, 56
forgotten, 56
fought, 52
freeze, 60
froze, 60
frozen, 60
gave, 62
get, 106
give, 62
given, 62
go, 107
gone, 107
got, 106
gotten, 106

grew, 109
grind, 108
ground, 108
grow, 109
grown, 109
had, 111
hang, 110
have, 111
held, 66
hid, 64
hidden, 64
hide, 64
hit, 112
hold, 66
hung, 110
hurt, 113
is, 12, 82
keep, 114
kept, 114
knew, 68
know, 68
known, 68
laid, 115
lain, 120
lay, 115, 120
lead, 116
leave, 117
led, 116
left, 117
lend, 118
lent, 118
let, 119
lie, 120
lose, 121
lost, 121
paid, 122
pay, 122
put, 123
ran, 129
rang, 127
read, 124
rid, 125
ridded, 125
ridden, 126
ride, 126
ring, 127
rise, 128
risen, 128
rode, 126
rose, 128
run, 129

rung, 127
said, 130
sang, 136
saw, 70
say, 130
see, 70
seek, 72
seen, 70
set, 131
shake, 74
shaken, 74
shine, 132
shined, 132
shone, 132
shook, 74
shoot, 133
shot, 133
show, 134
showed, 134
shown, 134
shrank, 135
shrink, 135
shrunk, 135
shrunken, 135
sing, 83, 136
slain, 137
slay, 137
sleep, 138
slept, 138
slew, 137
slid, 139
slide, 139
sought, 72
speak, 140
spin, 141
spoke, 140
spoken, 140
sprang, 142
spring, 142
sprung, 142
spun, 141
stand, 143
stank, 146
steal, 144
stick, 145
sting, 76
stink, 146
stole, 144
stolen, 144
stood, 143
stricken, 147

stridden, 146
stride, 146
strike, 147
strive, 148
strived, 148
striven, 146
strode, 146
strove, 148
struck, 147
stuck, 145
stung, 76
stunk, 146
sung, 83, 136
swam, 150
swear, 149
swim, 150
swing, 78
swore, 149
sworn, 149
swum, 150
swung, 78
take, 151
taken, 151
taught, 80
teach, 80
tear, 152
think, 153
thought, 153
threw, 154
throw, 154
thrown, 154
took, 151
tore, 152
torn, 152
wake, 155
waked, 155
was, 12, 82
wear, 156
went, 107
were, 12, 82
woke, 155
woken, 155
wore, 156
worn, 156
wring, 157
write, 158
written, 158
wrote, 158
wrung, 157